VITAL VOICES

VITAL VOICES

THE POWER OF WOMEN LEADING CHANGE AROUND THE WORLD

Alyse Nelson

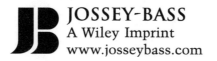

JOSSEY-BASS
A Wiley Imprint
www.josseybass.com

Published by Jossey-Bass
A Wiley Imprint
One Montgomery Street, Suite 1200, San Francisco, CA 94104-4594—www.josseybass.com

Jossey-Bass books and products are available through most bookstores. To contact Jossey-Bass directly call our Customer Care Department within the U.S. at 800-956-7739, outside the U.S. at 317-572-3986, or fax 317-572-4002.

Wiley publishes in a variety of print and electronic formats and by print-on-demand. Some material included with standard print versions of this book may not be included in e-books or in print-on-demand. If this book refers to media such as a CD or DVD that is not included in the version you purchased, you may download this material at http://booksupport.wiley.com. For more information about Wiley products, visit www.wiley.com.

Library of Congress Cataloging-in-Publication Data
Nelson, Alyse, 1974–
    Vital voices : the power of women leading change around the world / Alyse Nelson. — 1st ed.
    p. cm.
    Includes bibliographical references and index.
    ISBN 978-1-118-18477-6 (cloth), 978-1-118-22750-3 (ebk), 978-1-118-24053-3 (ebk), 978-1-118-26511-6 (ebk)
 1.   Women—Political activity. 2.   Women social reformers. 3.   Leadership in women.
 4.   Social change. I. Title.
    HQ1236.N45 2012
    305.42—dc23

                                                                                    2012010376

Printed in the United States of America
FIRST EDITION
HB Printing 10 9 8 7 6 5 4 3 2 1

For the women whose voices have inspired, humbled, and propelled us forward and to those still struggling to have their voices heard

Photo Credits

CONTENTS

THE HONORABLE HILLARY RODHAM CLINTON

Founder, Vital Voices

IN 1995, DELEGATES FROM 189 NATIONS MET in Beijing for the United Nations Fourth World Conference on Women. I stood before those gathered and said the time had come to break our silence.

No longer would we accept any separation between women's rights and human rights. No longer would discussions about *"women's issues"* take place unnoticed, in back rooms.

Vital Voices began as a government initiative during the Clinton Administration at a time of great change in the world. Many countries were emerging from conflict and repression, beginning the transition to democracy. Former Secretary and my friend, Madeleine Albright, and I, along with others at the State Department and the White House, believed it was critical that women have a role in shaping the futures that they would inhabit. We believed that if women were brave enough and strong enough to challenge the status quo and participate in politics, civil society, the economy, we should help them.

An idea that began in a small office at the State Department as the Vital Voices Democracy Initiative has grown into Vital Voices Global Partnership, an NGO with more than one thousand staff and partners worldwide, supporting the work of twelve thousand women leaders in 144 countries.

This organization and its mission are very close to my heart. I carry the lessons of Vital Voices with me every day. At the State Department, we are working hard to embed support for women's rights and advancement as a cornerstone of U.S. foreign policy. Melanne Verveer, the co-founder of Vital Voices, is leading that effort as our Ambassador-at-Large for Global Women's Issues. And everywhere I go in the world, somebody from Vital Voices comes to see me. They tell me about a training program or a visit, an opportunity they had to advance their work even further.

Since 1995, it has become very clear that development stalls where women are oppressed, and accelerates where they are empowered.

We know that women make unique and critical contributions. They often see problems that others overlook. They are able to reach populations that others either cannot reach or do not care to do. And even when it seems that no opportunity exists, they still find a way.

The status of the world's women is not only a matter of morality and justice. It is also a political, economic, and social imperative. Put simply, the world cannot make lasting progress if women and girls in the twenty-first century are denied their rights and left behind.

The women leaders you will meet in the pages of this book hail from different cultures and parts of the world, but they share important values and attributes. They each look for ways to make systemic change—to lift the lives of thousands, even millions of people.

These women embody a distinct, transformative model of leadership. After 15 years of experience, we know the multiplying effect we achieve when we invest in women who embody this model. Their actions initiate a positive chain reaction that quickly acquires an energy of its own.

At a time when millions of women worldwide are still denied their rights, still excluded from the public debates in their societies, still subjected to violence inside and outside of the family, still barred from schools, courts, markets, and public squares, it is even more remarkable that these women persevere.

Their courage has inspired others to stand with them despite the risks and the consequences—to believe in the possibility of a better future and their own ability to help build it. We must proclaim to the world, clearly and as one, that these women are heroes, their work is valuable, and their voices are vital.

This is not only an urgent foreign policy challenge. It is not simply a social justice issue, the most important in my view for the twenty-first century. It is a personal mission. And I am deeply honored to recognize and pay gratitude to those women who are on the front lines across the world who make each of us dare a little more, risk a little more, do a little more.

INTRODUCTION

IN OCTOBER 2008, WHEN THE GLOBAL ECONOMIC meltdown was on the front page of every newspaper, a story caught my attention; it was, quite possibly, the first solution-oriented story I'd seen about the crisis. After declaring bankruptcy, the government of Iceland tapped two women to rebuild the financial system. A government official noted that after the banking empire collapsed, "women are taking over ... to clean it up."[1] Audur Capital, which is managed solely by women, was the only private equity fund untouched by the crisis[2]; and in the midst of economic chaos, Icelanders elected Johanna Sigurdardottir—a woman—as prime minister.

As I read on, I thought the solution to the situation in Iceland made perfect sense. Through my work with Vital Voices, I know firsthand countless stories of women leading the charge throughout the world. There are the women of Rwanda, who rose from the ashes of genocide to rebuild their country, which as of 2011 boasted the only female-majority parliament in the world[3] and one of Africa's fastest-growing GDPs.[4] Or the young congresswoman in Peru, who at the tender age of twenty-eight publicly demanded an account for the increase in poverty and human rights violations perpetrated with impunity during Alberto Fujimori's regime. There are many stories like this in every region, country, and community of the world—stories of women stepping up as leaders in times of crisis, whether financial, humanitarian, or otherwise.

For generations, women around the world have been pleading for equality on grounds of fairness. After all, women make up slightly more than half the global population. While these sentiments and the language of fairness bolster the argument for justice, there are more broadly compelling reasons for women's full participation. As women gain greater access and opportunities, their collective participation generates a kind of societal change unlike anything the world has ever seen. In some of the most difficult times, in many of the most dangerous places, women are taking on and chipping away at the world's most serious problems.

The people of Iceland weren't the only ones making the connection between women and economic development. A few months earlier, in March 2008, Goldman Sachs's chairman and CEO, Lloyd Blankfein, had announced the historic investment of $100 million over five years to provide women in emerging markets with a business and management education—an initiative they call "10,000 Women." This commitment was preceded by Goldman Sachs's "Women Hold Up Half the Sky" report, which made an economic argument for investing in women of the developing world.[5] More impressive than the size of the gift was the clear and visible commitment from the top. Goldman Sachs saw this not only as the right thing to do; they understood that it was a smart investment in the sustainability of their business.

At the launch event at Columbia University in New York, I looked out at the enthusiastic crowd: women—but also, a sea of men in dark suits. *Clearly*, I thought, *a new day has come.*

· · ·

Back in 1995, when I first started working on global women's issues, the constituency for these issues was not so broad. You couldn't read Nicholas Kristof's impassioned *New York Times* columns highlighting international heroines on the front lines of change. There were few books or articles written on the topic. We had no language, and very little research to speak of, to articulate the critical role of women in building a better world. On the contrary, most news stories depicted women as victims or vessels, in need of pity or protection. Up until the United Nations Fourth World Conference on Women in Beijing, China, where then–First Lady Hillary Clinton proclaimed, "women's rights are human rights," women's issues had been tangential, at best, to the foreign policy agendas of most governments.

Only a few brave voices had made the case for the advancement of women as a path to development and democracy. Harvard professor and World Bank economist Larry Summers' 1994 study, *Investing in All the People: Educating Women in Developing Countries,* highlighted the increased economic returns from investing in girls' education.[6] Nobel Prize-winning economist Amartya Sen argued that nothing was more important to the development of nations than the contributions of women. Even in 1995, with just a few influential advocates and little data, it was clear to some that in a new era of globalization, countries would find it difficult to make economic or social progress if 50 percent of their people—their greatest natural resource—remained untapped and held back from contributing at their full potential.

Just like Sen and Summers, Hillary Clinton saw that investing in the untapped potential of the world's women was the quickest route to advancing sustainable peace, democracy, and economic development. In 1997, fueled by the energy of 55,000 women leaders from around the world gathered at the UN Conference on Women in Beijing, the First Lady returned home to the United States, and with then–Secretary of State Madeleine Albright initiated the Vital Voices Democracy Initiative within the State Department. The mission was bold: to promote the advancement of women's leadership as a U.S. foreign policy goal, and to make visible the connection that those states promoting women's rights were the same states exhibiting an unwavering commitment to democratic and progressive ideals. In the late 1990s, this was a radical concept.

More than a decade after Vital Voices' founding, Secretary of State Hillary Clinton routinely addresses the intertwined nature of women's rights and U.S. foreign policy. Challenges once sidelined as "women's issues" have moved into the mainstream, especially with the world's attention focused on economic recovery and development. This makes sense, given that women, collectively, are the fastest-growing economic force in the world, controlling over $20 trillion in spending globally.[7] The Asia Pacific region alone would gain

$42–$47 billion per year if women had greater access to job opportunities.[8]

The reality is that women's progress is global progress. In societies where women have equal access to education and political rights, governments are more open and free, and younger generations are healthier and better educated. The United Nations has found that women in developing nations reinvest up to 90 percent of their income in their families and communities, as opposed to the 30–40 percent that men reinvest.[9]

From a development standpoint, women are what economists call a growth reserve, meaning that there is still tremendous economic potential that has gone untapped. *The Economist* estimates that over the past couple of decades, women have contributed more to global GDP growth than have new technologies or emerging economic heavyweights India and China.[10] The United Nations finds that women do 66 percent of the world's work[11], and for the first time in history, as of 2010 women constitute a majority of the workforce in the United States.[12] Businesses and governments alike are formulating strategies to channel women's energy to generate prosperity for all.

Simply stated, women have become the emerging market. And that brings some new players to the table. As recently as 2005, if someone had asked me what I thought would be the fastest, most effective way to advance women and girls globally, I would have said it was for governments to turn their rhetoric on these issues into measurable action. Of course, government action is still sorely needed, yet I've come to understand that the private sector can be just as powerful. When corporations enter the ring, aligning their philanthropic endeavors with their core business strategies, they can change the game for women in the communities where they operate. Companies have the incentive and the reach to inspire a cultural shift that positively impacts the lives and livelihoods of women and their families, and that sends a powerful message to governments and citizens about the value of women.

Each year more corporations announce large-scale initiatives to capitalize on women's untapped economic potential. In 2011, Coca-Cola's chairman and CEO, Muhtar Kent, unveiled his company's "5 by 20 Initiative" to provide economic opportunities to five million women by 2020. And that same year, Walmart launched their "360 Initiative," the largest, multibillion dollar corporate commitment to date, to buy products for the company's supply chain from women-owned businesses around the world. Media titan Tina Brown has boldly used her platform at *Newsweek* and *The Daily Beast* to channel new attention to women's organizations.

These are indisputable signs of progress. Those of us working on global women's issues have a new vocabulary, a growing body of research, and greater understanding. We have more partners and more advocates than ever before. In 2007, World Bank president Robert Zoellick declared gender equality as "smart economics," launching a four-year gender action plan to increase women's access to land and greater economic participation.[13] Two years later, President Barack Obama appointed Melanne Verveer, Vital Voices co-founder and chair emeritus, as the first ever ambassador-at-large for Global Women's Issues, with a direct line to the secretary of state. And a few years after that, he made history with the first Executive Order instituting a National Action Plan on Women, Peace and Security to rally the U.S. government around the critical role that women play in building peace and preventing conflict.[14]

In 2010 the United Nations created "UN Women" to accelerate gender equality and hold member states accountable; former Chilean President Michelle Bachelet was appointed as its first leader. And the following year, former French finance minister Christine Lagarde was the overwhelming choice to lead the International Monetary Fund, becoming the first woman to head a multilateral financial institution. Leaders across the globe have condemned violence against women for its devastating impact on individuals, communities, societies, and even the economy. And multilateral institutions have linked women's participation in the political process to good governance.

Yet with all of the progress, there is still a long way to go. Women's full economic potential is far from realized. A majority of the world's women do not legally own, control, or inherit property, land, or wealth.[15] Women have less access to credit, education and training, technology, markets, mentors, networks, and protection under the law.[16] Too frequently, as a result, they are unable to start and grow small businesses. As of 2012, women-owned businesses represent less than 1 percent of sales to large, multinational corporations.[17] Notwithstanding their constituting a majority of university students globally, women's formal labor force participation hovers around 51 percent globally, as opposed to men's at

78 percent.[18] Even the economic advances of women will only be sustainable if they are reinforced by increased access to social and political opportunity.

The United Nations estimates that 603 million women live in countries where domestic violence is not considered a crime.[19] Staggeringly, one out of every three women in the world will be a victim of violence in her lifetime.[20] Although two-thirds of countries around the world have laws in place to combat violence against women, in most cases those laws are rarely enforced, well resourced, or even taken seriously.[21] Violence against women and girls—in the forms of human trafficking, harmful cultural practices, rape as a tactic of war, and domestic violence—is one of the single greatest factors holding women back. If we as global citizens don't address the inequity of restricted access or the scourge of gender-based violence, women's potential will go unrealized and whole communities will stand to lose. In fact, in environments where women get an equitable share, opportunities and prosperity are increased for all.

Vital Voices was established with that premise in mind, that improving one group's access to opportunity doesn't mean denying possibility to another. At the dawn of the millennium, Vital Voices left the State Department and became a nonpartisan, nonprofit, nongovernmental organization, rebranding itself as the Vital Voices Global Partnership. Then Senator Hillary Clinton reached across the political aisle to engage Republican Senator Kay Bailey Hutchison and former Republican Senator Nancy Kassebaum Baker in this mission, and together they became our honorary cochairs. Though we were blessed with an impressive and influential, bipartisan board of directors, I was the NGO's first and, for a short time, only employee. Between 2000 and 2012, our staff grew to more than fifty. In our first fifteen years, we worked with over twelve thousand women leaders from 144 countries. And though we set out hoping to better the lives of women, as it turns out, it was the women we met who bettered us.

In the beginning, our goal was to get more women to the decision-making table. We identified the women in each community who were leaders in the areas of economic opportunity, political participation, and human rights, and we worked to amplify their voices and bolster their efforts to make change. We offered training, networking, and mentorship programs to equip women with new skills and contacts. We brought issue experts together with on-the-ground practitioners to identify solutions to challenges; Vital Voices programs were international events that convened some of the best and the bravest in every region. We were especially proud when women leaders began taking practical models from one region and replicating them in another. But the greatest impact of our work was something we hadn't envisioned. When the leaders left our programs and returned home, they began training others on what they had learned. We realized that women leaders are multipliers. Through them, our impact could be exponential. Their efforts have become central to Vital Voices' success.

Paying it forward—using power to empower others— was just one in a series of traits we observed in the many women leaders we came to know, traits that taken together have expanded the way we view leadership. These qualities are taking root and gaining attention as more women attain positions of influence around the world. We believe these traits represent a potential sea change in the way people interact. Women's economic potential is extraordinary, but may be surpassed by their contribution to society as inclusive and collaborative leaders.

This book will take you on a journey that spans seventeen years, from the United Nations' Beijing women's conference in 1995 to the world of 2012, across continents and countries, from remote villages to sprawling cities. You will witness the early days of Vital Voices and the women who shaped us, how this organization first came together and then built upon its early iteration to become fully independent of government ties as a leading nonprofit. Through the stories of the women driving this movement, you will learn what we at Vital Voices have learned: that contemporary women leaders around the world are building a different model of leadership, one that we believe can be uniquely effective in tackling many of humanity's most pressing challenges.

The women we work with are phenomenally diverse, representing a range of backgrounds and experience. Yet across their differences, we've found that the fabric of their leadership is woven from common threads:

- A driving force or sense of mission
- Strong roots in the community
- An ability to connect across lines that divide
- Bold ideas and bold action
- A resolve to pay it forward

Each chapter of this book shines a spotlight on one of these leadership traits. We do not view the traits as distinct or sequential, but rather as mutually reinforcing. Moreover, while Vital Voices has learned about the power of these leadership traits from women, this is not a model of, by, or for women only. Rather, we believe that this model is potent for everyone in today's world. As globalization proceeds, as technology spreads, and as communities get bigger, the need for more collaborative and inclusive leadership is increasingly clear. As nations around the world struggle to recover from the financial crisis, we need to rethink the status quo and tap women's full potential, not just as drivers of economic growth but in bringing forth a new model of leadership.

In our view, and as the final chapter explores, leadership is a journey, not a destination. More than any title, rank, or status, leadership is about the actions we take on a daily basis, the way we choose to live our lives, and the responsibility we take for the well-being of the world we share. We fervently believe that anyone can choose leadership and have a positive impact on others' lives.

Through Vital Voices, we have learned much from watching and working with extraordinary leaders in action, and from seeing how they've used their experiences to drive progress. What we have learned has made us a better organization, better able to support and stand behind other women around the world. Our goal, with this book, is to share those lessons as widely as we can in the hopes that other women—and all individuals—who aspire to make a difference can draw inspiration, guidance, and hope from these voices, their stories, and their successes.

VITAL
VOICES

CHAPTER ONE

A DRIVING FORCE OR SENSE OF MISSION

INTRODUCED BY THE HONORABLE MICHELLE BACHELET

Under-Secretary General and Executive Director, UN Women

EXPERIENCE HAS TAUGHT ME THAT THERE IS no limit to what women can accomplish. A sense of mission compels me to believe in the possible. The quest for peace, human rights, dignity, and equality, which guides the work of the United Nations and UN Women, provides a sense of mission to millions of women and men around the world. We are united in a common cause for freedom and justice.

A leader always looks to the future. This does not mean forgetting about the past. On the contrary, the need for a better society is derived from lessons learned. In building a democratic nation, one builds on the past, moving forward with a sense of mission for a future that includes everyone and ensures rights and opportunities for all.

When I was minister of defense in Chile, before I became president, my mission was to further reform the defense sector and continue working to ensure the rule of law. During the military regime, human rights had been violated and the military was a symbol of fear for the people. By approaching this duty with hope instead of anger, it was possible to support the people and the armed forces to move forward in a spirit of national identity and determination. We were driven by a shared sense of mission to overcome authoritarianism by creating institutions to uphold democratic values.

Democracy is rooted in peace and justice, and democratic reform requires leadership with conviction.

Those who lead with conviction include the women you will come to know in this chapter—Marina Pisklakova, Hafsat Abiola, Anel Townsend Diez-Canseco, Sunitha Krishnan, and Dr. Hawa Abdi. They can and do realize extraordinary accomplishments. As I always say, the most important thing is to never give up. Democracy, justice, and peace demand the full and equal participation of women. Justice is a long-term undertaking.

During my life, I have had the privilege to live in service of shared goals for democracy, equality, and justice, first for my country of Chile, and now for the women of our world through UN Women, the first United Nations agency dedicated to advancing women's empowerment and gender equality.

I continue on my journey with hope.

I had to go. In August 1995, all I could think about was the United Nations Fourth World Conference on Women in Beijing, China—widely predicted to be the largest-ever gathering of women leaders and activists in history. Women from every corner of the globe were expected to attend, representing different generations, religions, cultures, socioeconomic backgrounds, and professions; all united around one common goal: improving the status of women in our world.

I was twenty-one years old at the time, coming of age in an increasingly interconnected world and desperate to understand my place within it as an American woman. I saved and borrowed money and bought the cheapest airline ticket I could find, one involving four layovers before touching down in Beijing. As it turned out, buying the ticket was the easy part.

After I'd mailed in my registration forms, photograph, and $50 application fee, the Chinese Organizing Committee denied my request for a conference visa. For two straight weeks, I went to the Chinese Consulate in Los Angeles every morning, demanding an explanation. Later, I learned that more than a third of those who registered for the conference were never granted visas. A young Chinese consular officer took pity on me, or maybe just grew tired of my visits, and suggested that I apply for a tourist visa under the guise of a traveling student. Once I had made it to China, he thought I'd be able to get into the conference itself.

Tourist visa in hand, I reserved two nights at a hotel in Beijing I couldn't afford, telling myself I would figure something out when I arrived. It would be an adventure—and though I didn't know it then, a life-changing experience.

For me, the conference began on the last leg of my journey into Beijing. The plane was filled with women attending the conference, including my seatmate, a warm and enthusiastic human rights activist from South Africa named Gertrude Fester. She seemed so upbeat that I was sobered later to learn that she had been arrested and imprisoned for nearly three years because of her efforts to fight apartheid.

Gertrude had followed the UN's world conferences on women since the inaugural gathering in Mexico City in 1975. She told me how, at the time, the issue of domestic violence wasn't recognized as a public issue. It was seen as a private issue, not to be discussed outside the home, but women around the world were talking about "the problem that had no name." At the third UN Conference in Nairobi, Kenya, in 1985, advocates pushed to have domestic violence included in the official document coming out of the conference. "We each returned to our home countries pointing to the fact that our government and nearly every other nation in the world recognized it as a problem," Gertrude explained. "From that place of authority, we started pushing for legislation to outlaw domestic violence."

The Beijing conference would be the fourth in the series. I learned from Gertrude that official delegations planned to join in signing on to a "Platform for Action" to improve the lives of women in twelve critical areas, from health to economic status to political participation. Meanwhile, as many as forty thousand nongovernmental leaders, advocates, and activists would gather for the parallel NGO Forum in Huairou, a sleepy northern suburb.

The more I learned, the more I realized that this would truly be a historic gathering. Still, I knew my participation wasn't guaranteed. I confided in Gertrude about my awkward visa situation, and my fears that I would be turned away. "Well," she said, leaning back confidently in her seat, "we can fix that."

As we left the plane and collected our luggage, a flock of enthusiastic students holding signs with the forum logo ushered women onto buses headed to Huairou. Gertrude and I attempted to board, but I didn't make it far. A nervous young woman checking passports at the door alerted her superior, who told me I could not join the group because I did not have a proper visa. In an act of sisterly solidarity, Gertrude disembarked as well, as if to say, don't worry, we will figure this out together. We took a taxi to a hotel in Beijing for the night, and plotted our next step. The following day, we returned to the airport and scoped out the convoy of buses once again.

This time, we made a detour and Gertrude headed toward the road, dragging me and her suitcase in tow. She led me about a quarter of a mile, just beyond the sights of the officials. Soon we saw a bus heading toward the conference. Without warning, Gertrude jumped out onto the road right in the path of the oncoming bus.

"Stop!" she shouted. "We are all sisters!"

The bus screeched to a halt; the doors opened and we climbed on, to the surprise of the Russian delegates inside. Gertrude greeted each of them with a "Thank you very much," as she led the way to some open seats in the back. From Gertrude, I learned how to get things done.

The Chinese government's decision to move the conclave of nongovernmental leaders from Beijing out to the countryside was motivated, in part, by their desire to shelter the citizens of the capital city from what they imagined would be converging activists and radicals. I later discovered that taxi drivers throughout Beijing kept white sheets on hand for the duration of the conference, in case, I was told, any attendees decided to strip naked and march in the streets.

It took about an hour to get to Huairou. Local farmers and their families lined the road to watch the convoy coming to town. Finally, a barracks-like series of hastily built dormitories came into view. Our bus rolled up at the registration building. This was the moment of truth. As I waited in line to pick up my badge, my heart was pounding and I had to catch my breath just to tell the young woman my name. She examined my passport. Flustered, she called for help. After a few minutes one of her colleagues came back and said, "You need to go into Beijing and register there."

"I've been there." (I had been told by my consulate friend in Los Angeles that the authorities wouldn't want a jilted young feminist hanging out on the streets for ten days; that it was likely they would let me in on the spot to avoid greater protests.) "They told me that I should come here to register and pick up my badge." A few minutes later, the young woman returned, my badge in hand—complete with the photograph of myself I'd sent in with my registration.

I reunited with Gertrude, who was just as excited as I was at the sight of that precious badge. "Beautiful, my dear, beautiful!" One of her friends had taken one look at the stark dormitories and decided to stay elsewhere. Gertrude snatched the housing form out of her hand, put it in mine, and said, "And now you have a place to sleep, my dear."

The Chinese Organizing Committee had decided to separate women by region: the Eastern Europeans with the Eastern Europeans, the women from Latin America together, another set of buildings for the women from the Middle East. With my borrowed papers, I found myself in a tiny dorm room with two African women.

I learned that one of them was from Eritrea and the other from Ethiopia, two countries that had been at war for decades. Despite the differences in their backgrounds and perspectives, they immediately started looking for points of connection and commonality—their children, their families, their work. Watching them together was fascinating.

After dinner, hundreds of women loaded into buses to ride into Beijing for the spectacular opening ceremonies featuring speakers and performances from around the world. The African women wore handmade, embroidered dresses in vibrant colors—some adorned with intertwining symbols of the UN peace dove and the universal woman symbol. My bus was just one of what seemed like a few hundred buses full of women activists. Suddenly, I felt very small. These women hadn't come to Beijing to understand their place in this world. They came here to fight for it.

• • •

The African women were buzzing over breakfast the next day. Aung San Suu Kyi was to deliver the opening keynote address. Perhaps the best-known political prisoner since Nelson Mandela, she had recently been released by the military dictatorship after nearly six years of house arrest. Though no longer under guard, she couldn't leave Burma without running the risk of being denied reentry. So a video of her speech had been smuggled out to Beijing.

Suu's father, the great general Aung San, was a hero of Burma's fight for independence. In 1947, when Suu was just two years old, her father was assassinated by political rivals. As a teenager, her family moved to India, where her mother served as Burma's ambassador. Later, while studying at Oxford, she met and married Michael Aris, a British scholar; they had two sons. She rarely returned to Burma during those years except for holidays. Still, she could not forget her people and would often tell her husband that one day she would return if they needed her. That day came in 1988.

Suu was in Burma nursing her dying mother just as prodemocracy protests broke out. After twenty-six years, General Ne Win had stepped down as chairman of the Burma Socialist Party. Mass demonstrations for democracy were brutally suppressed by the military, and nearly four thousand Burmese people were killed.[1] At a rally of an estimated one million Burmese citizens at the Shwedagon Pagoda in Yangon, Aung San Suu Kyi took the stage, calling for a new democratic government. As her father's daughter, she had the attention of the entire nation.

Nevertheless, a new military junta took power the next month. In response to the military's ensuing violence and oppression, a political party, the National League for Democracy (NLD), was formed, and Aung San Suu Kyi became its general secretary. Like her father, she aimed to help her people achieve a "second independence," this time from military rule. But she was determined to bring about change through nonviolent means.

In 1989, Aung San Suu Kyi was detained under martial law without charge or trial. Even in detention, she connected with the people of Burma, who were hungry for democracy and for a fair and just society. When the regime allowed elections in 1990, the NLD won 81 percent of the seats in the National Assembly, even with the leader of the party under house arrest.[2] The junta annulled the election results and refused to hand over power. Aung San Suu Kyi was offered her freedom if she would agree to leave Burma. She declined, even though it meant she might never see her sons or her husband again.

The treatment of Aung San Suu Kyi was internationally condemned. In 1990, she was awarded the Rafto Memorial Prize and the Sakharov Prize for Freedom of Thought, and in 1991 she became the eighth woman to receive the Nobel Peace Prize. The Nobel Committee's chairman declared, "Aung San Suu Kyi brings out something of the best in us. We feel we need precisely her sort of person in order to retain our faith in the future. That is what gives her such power as a symbol, and that is why any ill treatment of her feels like a violation of what we have most at heart."[3]

• • •

Although the video in Beijing was grainy and the sound slightly muffled, Suu's message was clear. She spoke about tolerance and inclusion, and how women bring these values to the world. She highlighted women's ability to defuse conflict through dialogue, rather than by resorting to vengeance or violence. And she spoke of her own responsibility to strive for the release and the return of those who continued to suffer for a democratic future that she had helped to champion.

As a young feminist, I was mesmerized by her quiet strength. She was intently focused on her vision for Burma's future. It seemed nothing could diminish her sense of purpose, or rob her of her conviction; she spoke with clarity and focus, inspiring others not to give up hope.

This was the first time I had been exposed to leadership based on moral legitimacy rather than official authority. Aung San Suu Kyi was the elected leader of her country, and yet she had spent the last five years confined to her home. Stripped of her freedom, let alone the ability to govern, she was still more powerful than the junta, because she had something they would never have: the hearts and minds of the people.

Fellow Nobel Laureate Archbishop Desmond Tutu has said when speaking of Daw Suu: "The people are not stupid. They know who are their real leaders. You can throw them in prison. You can ban them. You can send them into exile, but the people will always know, 'Those are our leaders.'" The people of Burma certainly knew. Daw Suu started a movement that has sustained the hope of her people for more than two decades.

As enthralled as I was by Suu's words, I was also acutely aware of the reactions from the women around me. They all seemed to have an unwavering sense of purpose, a focus and determination that gave them energy against the odds. These were qualities that easily transcended culture or geography, and seemed to me to form the bedrock of women's leadership. Soon, I would see an example from my own country that reaffirmed this ideal.

• • •

On the final day of the conference I woke up before dawn and joined the thousands of other women headed to the amphitheater where U.S. First Lady Hillary Rodham Clinton was to speak. Back in Washington, D.C., it was no secret that many were unhappy about the First Lady's participation in the Beijing women's conference and parallel NGO Forum. For months leading up to the conference, U.S. government officials had debated about whether it would be "appropriate" for the First Lady to speak at a human rights conference in China, given the country's poor human rights record—including its treatment of women and girls. For instance, the practice of infanticide or sex-selected abortion was a widespread response to the country's one-child policy; 100 million baby girls were "missing" from the popluation.[4]

When Mrs. Clinton was named honorary chairwoman of the U.S. delegation to the conference, her attendance became fodder for the 1996 presidential campaign. From the presidential campaign trail, Republican Senator Bob Dole announced that he didn't see any "useful purpose" in her trip, particularly since China was holding an American

11

human rights activist, Harry Wu, as a political prisoner.[5] Even within President Clinton's own staff, officials could not agree whether the First Lady should go. The only one who seemed certain was the First Lady herself. As she later wrote in her memoir, *Living History*, "I sympathized with their cause, but it disappointed me that, once again, the crucial concerns of women might be sacrificed."[6]

In the eleventh hour, Harry Wu was released from prison and the White House approved the First Lady's trip. Pundits speculated about a last-minute diplomatic quid pro quo, in which the Chinese had agreed to release Wu if Mrs. Clinton would refrain from criticizing the government. This was not the case. Mrs. Clinton was clear that she would not be deterred from her purpose in going to Beijing: speaking truth on the rights of women everywhere in the world.

As I stood in the dark, early morning hours, the queue of women waiting for Hillary grew. The theater could hold only a few hundred people, but I was standing near the front, and I was certain that I would be able to enter. But the hours ticked by, and the throng of women and I could only watch as a number of U.S. delegation members arrived; then members of the media, followed by Chinese government officials. Only a handful of spectators were allowed in before a Chinese Organizing Committee official announced that all the seats in the theater were full.

Most of the women at the conference never saw Mrs. Clinton at the podium. Only a fortunate few, including me, got to hear her remarks in real time, in rooms aside the theater, where the audio was piped in. But even in a pre–social media era, the First Lady's message spread like wildfire. Her speech in Beijing was electrifying for its focus and its forcefulness. With moral certainty, she cut through the vagueness of official language, laying a course towards women's full participation that changed the game for all players.

She spoke about the particular ways that women come together and share ideas. She spoke about how work performed by women is too often overlooked and uncounted in both public and private spaces. And then she proclaimed, "It is no longer acceptable to discuss women's rights as separate from human rights."

Jaws dropped. In China, in Washington, all around the world. At a time when recognizing women as equal and worthy human beings seemed a radical notion, something yet to be decided—or summarily denied—Mrs. Clinton's declaration was a clarion call, one that perfectly captured what the women at the conference felt. Women should not have to beg for the right to be safe and secure, to enjoy freedom of expression and equal access to opportunity. Women, as human beings, are entitled to these basic rights. And when governments classified the particular challenges faced by women as a special category of "extra" rights, it was just a way of relegating those challenges to a kind of special-interest limbo.

Mrs. Clinton brought that hypocrisy into sharp relief before every government represented in the room. Her words became a rallying cry among the activists assembled. Scores of women have told me since that they returned to their countries armed with the phrase "Women's rights are human rights," strengthened by the power behind those words.

From China's perspective, the First Lady's message was an embarrassing breach of protocol, drawing attention to the host country's human rights abuses. At home, she was criticized for making foreign policy statements beyond her authority to do so. But for those of us who had traveled to Beijing, the First Lady was a shining beacon of light. She had precisely identified the struggles women faced, and had articulated them before the entire world, demanding that the world take notice.

Though at the time she was not an elected official herself, she understood that she had a platform from which her message would be heard, a position that could not be ignored. She knew the power of her voice, and she used it to speak out for those whose voices were silenced.

· · ·

All the women who made indelible impressions on me in Beijing—from Gertrude and my African roommates to Aung San Suu Kyi and Hillary Clinton—were cause-driven leaders. Each had a strong vision for what she wanted to accomplish, and an unwavering commitment to that vision. They had journeyed to Beijing to find new ways to move those visions forward, and they infused every roundtable, speech, and conversation with clear, focused direction.

In the personal encounters I had with Gertrude and my roommates, I was struck by how vividly they embodied some of the common traits in women's leadership—the capacity to lift up others and reach across lines that commonly divide us. In listening to Aung San Suu Kyi, I was in awe of her readiness to sacrifice her freedom and safety for what she believed to be right. She saw beyond personal risk, beyond persecution, beyond enforced indignity, to stand up for the principles of nonviolence, equality, democracy, and justice. She held firm to her belief in a better future—knowing that a world built on a foundation of injustice cannot stand. And when I think of Mrs. Clinton's participation in Beijing, I can't help but admire her certitude. Even before it was clear she could go, she was adamant that she had to be there. When protocol dictated that she choose her words carefully, she instead spoke honestly about abysmal human rights records. When she had the world's attention, she used that opportunity to give credence and validation to the ongoing contributions of women in every village, town, and city around the world. She knew exactly what she was there to do, and she used her power to lift up and to empower others.

My experience in Beijing taught me the first lessons in leadership that would change my life's trajectory. True leaders, I learned, have heart and noble purpose. They draw strength from within to effect change in the wider world.

At Vital Voices, we call this internal compass a *driving force*. For some, it is a personal mission statement. It is the reason for getting up after being knocked down. It inspires and humbles you simultaneously, providing focus in the face of great adversity *and* great success. It is a force so strong that nothing and no one can distract you or deter you from your path.

Leaders like Aung San Suu Kyi can often seem as if they were destined for leadership. But most leaders are not *born*; they're *made* from opportunity and experience. Statistically, in almost every country of the world, women come into leadership later in life than men.[7] Women often find their voices as leaders through a series of events and experiences that change the way they see the world. For some, their driving force may be formed in one defining moment that has served as a call to action; for others it may be a traumatic event that they are able to turn around into a powerful force for good; for still others it is a series of small events that add up over time to something life-changing. But by the time the most effective women rise to leadership positions, they have already cultivated a deeply held conviction. They become leaders because they know what they have to do—and they feel compelled to act on it.

Indeed, most of the leaders with whom Vital Voices works, like the inspiring women in the examples below, describe their own driving force as something that took hold of them so fundamentally that they had no choice but to embrace it, and follow wherever it required them to go.

MARINA PISKLAKOVA
Russia

"I think for me, there is not one moment that I can point to and say that's when I knew that this was what I would commit my life to. Honestly speaking, I fell into it. A woman came to my Moscow office and said, 'I'm afraid that my husband will kill me, and no one will know.' At that time in Russia, there was no name for domestic violence. Women were suffering silently. They were invisible and had no voice."

When I think of the founding mothers of Vital Voices, I think of Marina Pisklakova. In 1997, Marina was a member of the Russian delegation of women handpicked by the U.S. embassy in Moscow to attend the first Vital Voices in Democracy conference in Vienna, Austria. The collapse of the Soviet Union was still fresh. Democracy and free-market economies were just starting to take root. Swanee Hunt, the terrific maverick U.S. ambassador to Austria at the time, had traveled across the region, where she saw the changes unfold, and she was struck by an idea. Like Mrs. Clinton, she believed that democracy would not flourish unless women's voices were heard. So she decided to bring together emerging women leaders from across the former Soviet bloc with women from Europe and the United States. The U.S. government-sponsored conference highlighted the high cost of excluding women from economic, political, and social development throughout the region.

The participants in that first conference came from a wide spectrum of cultures and issue areas such as political participation, economic development, and human rights. Marina Pisklakova was identified for her efforts to speak out against the growing problem of domestic violence in Russia that, according to police, did not exist.

Marina's work had begun in 1993 while she was working as a researcher at the Russian Academy of Sciences. Her task was to measure the primary concerns of women across the country. Among thousands of responses to a survey she developed, she received two letters from women describing an issue that she could not classify. Marina knew that they were describing what we would now call domestic violence, but back then there was no word for it in Russian.

She spoke of her dilemma to two women she saw every day while dropping off her son at school, and they both confessed to her that they, too, had been victims of domestic violence—something she would never have guessed. She soon realized that this was a massive problem resting just below the surface of polite society. Women kept the abuse hidden out of shame and guilt or to protect their children.

Word of Marina's survey spread in quiet conversation between women, and before long, Marina was receiving calls from women across the country. She confesses that at the time she didn't know what she was doing or how she could help them. She knew she needed support and guidance.

As part of Marina's work with the research institute with the Russian Academy of Sciences, she traveled to Sweden. There she asked her Swedish colleagues to connect her with people working on the issue of domestic violence. That's how she met Ritva Holmstoron, the director of the Crisis Center for Women of Gothenburg. Marina told her what she had uncovered, the overwhelming data of women in abusive home situations. "I remember telling Ritva, who led the center, that when I returned back to Russia, I would try to decide whether I could really help." Ritva looked at Marina and said simply, "Do you think you have a choice? You know you have to, and you will."

So in a one-room office with a single telephone, Marina started the very first domestic violence hotline in Russia, which later became Center ANNA, National Center for the Prevention of Violence. She worked there alone for six months, taking calls and counseling individuals. Soon she started taking cases.

It was only a few months before Marina began receiving threats from the abusive husbands or partners of women she was helping. She knew she would get nowhere going to the police; domestic violence was considered a private family issue. As a single mother, Marina was scared—constantly weighing her safety and the safety of her son against the voices of these women—but there was no doubt in her mind that hers was a mission that could not be abandoned. As the ANNA Center grew, Marina became increasingly overwhelmed by the calls for help. She felt like she had opened Pandora's box. She thought, *This is not sustainable. Not for me and not for these women.* She needed something bigger.

Her initial strategy was to push for passage of an anti–domestic violence law. It had worked in other countries, but in Russia's political climate, she found it was unlikely to succeed. So she shifted her focus and started reaching out to law enforcement agencies within the framework of existing law—initiating trainings with police, prosecutors, and judges.

Though the police did not understand the epidemic of domestic violence as such, they had been frustrated with its symptoms—namely, murder cases, assaults, complaints—which they didn't recognize as patterns of abuse. Marina brought them together with crisis center counselors. She identified interested and compassionate police officers, prosecutors, and judges who would become allies and trainers. Step by step, they worked together to build trust and mutual commitment to fighting violence against women.

Yet even as the movement grew, Marina barely slept. No matter how hard she worked, she couldn't get ahead of the problem. Every hour, a woman in Russia was dying at the hands of a relative.[8] Behind every name there was a story. Too often it was the story of a woman desperate to be a perfect wife and mother. From the outside, the all too common view was that these women were somehow flawed and deserving of discipline. Marina knew she needed to shift the way that people perceived the issue and to increase awareness of domestic violence as a social problem in Russia.

In 1997, the ANNA Center launched a national education campaign called "There Is No Excuse for Domestic Violence." The campaign demonstrated that domestic violence wasn't a private concern, but a public problem. Marina reached out to survivors of domestic violence, offering hotlines and safe havens to which they could turn when violence occurred. The first time she saw a victim of domestic violence speak openly in a television interview about her experience was a milestone for Marina. The woman did not cover her face, and the audience did not blame her. Public education was working.

By 1999, Marina had established eleven crisis centers throughout Russia and a network of thirty-five organizations committed to combating domestic violence. Working in partnership with ANNA, the Russian Ministry of Social Affairs also began opening crisis centers and shelters, and ANNA formed a broader network that included not only NGOs but also state-run organizations. As of 2012, that network comprised more than 160 organizations. Beyond Russia's borders, the international women's movement has helped as well. International laws, such as the Beijing Platform and the Convention on the Elimination of All Forms of Discrimination Against Women (CEDAW), have served as important tools, as have international organizations like the American Bar Association.

When Marina began her work, her objective was to help one woman. Nearly two decades later, her center and its network of partners have helped more than 200,000 women. "I know now," she said, "that if I were to stop, perhaps retire, the work would not stop, it would continue. I imagine pushing a large boulder up a steep hill, and then one day that boulder begins to roll on its own. To me this is success."

Even in those early days in 1994, there was a force inside, driving Marina's work. "My driving force has always been to give the invisible a voice," she says. "It took hold of me and, as I was warned, I had no choice. It has been something that I have been trying to live up to for all these years."

HAFSAT ABIOLA
Nigeria

"I can remember the exact moment that it all came together for me. I was walking across the quad at Harvard in 1996. A group of students were collecting signatures for something. 'Oh, what is it this time?' I thought. 'Perhaps fighting for the right to walk barefoot in the quad?' But when they approached me, I realized they were collecting signatures to free an elected President in Africa from prison. They were talking about my father."

In 1993, Hafsat Abiola's father, Moshood Kahimawd Olawale Abiola, a successful, self-made businessman, was elected president of Nigeria on the platform, "Hope '93, Farewell to Poverty." The son of a poor farmer, Moshood Abiola was the first of his father's seventeen children to survive infancy. Known for his charisma and as a man of the people, he was a pioneer in philanthropy and believed that Africa should be a place of opportunity for all.

Nigeria had been under military rule for nearly thirty years, but in 1993 the military's ruling council had decided to hold democratic elections. Moshood Abiola won a landslide victory, setting in motion a prodemocracy movement that the military never anticipated. The election was swiftly annulled by the council, and Hafsat's father was incarcerated for having declared himself the winner. At the time, Hafsat had no interest in politics. She was planning to earn her PhD at Harvard and then return to Nigeria to do what her mother had done: get married and raise a family. But in 1993, everything changed.

When Hafsat's father was imprisoned, her mother, Kudirat Abiola, began campaigning for his release. Hafsat remembers rushing back from class for daily phone calls with her mother, who would relate her efforts to keep hope alive for democracy and to keep pressure on the military for Moshood's release. "What can I do to help?" Hafsat would ask. Her mother always replied, "The best thing you can do right now is to stay in school."

On the afternoon Hafsat was approached by those students, she realized that perhaps there was something she could do. Her impression of Americans, to that point, had been that they didn't know very much about anything going on in countries outside their own. But suddenly, here were Americans who cared about her father's plight, half a world away.

She rushed back to her dorm room to call her mother. "Mom, there are some students here on campus from Amnesty International. They are campaigning for Dad's release. They want to have me come and speak to some people about the situation. Mom, I think there is something I can do here to help."

Over the next few weeks, Kudirat coached her by phone, helping her daughter find her voice and the courage to speak in public. They both looked forward to Hafsat's graduation ceremony, when they would see each other for the first time in over a year. But then one day, Kudirat missed one of their regular calls. "I knew something wasn't right," Hafsat recalled, "but I assumed she was sick or that she got caught up with her activism work that day." An urgent call from family friends revealed the terrible truth: Kudirat had been assassinated—gunned down following a labor strike that she had helped to organize.

With her mother gone and her father still in prison, Hafsat felt she had no choice but to carry on their legacy. "I realized I had to be their voice," she says. "I started traveling across the United States speaking to church groups, student groups, politicians, corporate leaders—anyone who would listen and who would help my cause: the release of my father and the honoring of democracy."

I met Hafsat through a mutual friend in 1997. At the time, I was working at the State Department, and Hafsat had been pushing to meet with State Department officials to engage their support in calling for her father's release. By this time, she was an experienced and impressive advocate, a powerful and persuasive speaker who had incredible potential to bring change to her country. But what struck me most was her resilience, even after having experienced such tragic loss at a young age. With quiet intensity, she focused her energy on making change in Nigeria.

In 1998, Under Secretary of State Thomas Pickering and Assistant Secretary of State for African Affairs Susan Rice traveled to Nigeria to meet with Hafsat's father in prison and to encourage the military to allow a democratic election. On the eve of his scheduled release, Moshood Abiola collapsed in the presence of Pickering and Rice. Hafsat and her family believe Moshood was poisoned, though the official cause of death was given as a heart attack. The military government promptly announced democratic elections within nine months. "My parents never saw democracy come to Nigeria. They died for this cause."

After the deaths of her parents, many people asked Hafsat if she would carry on their political legacies. She clearly embodied the Abiola vision, charisma, and commitment, but her approach was more strategic. She told me, "in Nigeria we don't just need one or two good leaders—we need a sea change."

Three decades of military rule had fostered a dictatorial style of leadership in Nigeria. Hafsat explained, "Our government became synonymous with theft of public resources; $12 billion in oil revenues from 1988 to 1994 could not be accounted for,[9] likely doled out to those few in power." Despite its natural wealth, Nigeria had become one of the poorest countries in the world.[10] In 1999, the United Nations noted that two-thirds of Nigeria's population of more than 100 million people lived below the poverty line.[11] Life expectancy had dropped to fifty-three years, which is ten years below the average for developing countries;[12] and nearly half the population did not have access to clean drinking water and sanitation.[13] "The soldiers cannibalized the economy and they ruined us politically and psychologically," wrote Gbenga Adefaye, editor of the independent, Lagos-based *Vanguard* newspaper. "We are hoping to sort out our lives after they leave."[14]

Hafsat believes that Nigeria's women, who gained least and paid most under military rule, offer a strong possibility for change. They have preserved the culture of consensus, positive values, and partnership, and are therefore uniquely positioned to dismantle the violent political traditions that hinder democracy. Unfortunately, Nigerian women are rarely given the opportunity to hold positions of political leadership.

"Bad leadership has crushed the potential of my country. The best way to honor my parents' legacy is to be part of creating that sea of change—a new reality," Hafsat explained. In 1999, she founded the Kudirat Initiative for Democracy, KIND, to honor her mother by helping thousands find their voice. For over a decade, she has trained young women to play a leadership role in shaping the future of her country: "to lead we have to look for places where humanity is stuck and help fashion the lever that lifts us out of the rut we are in."

KIND trains young women to take responsibility for their personal and professional lives and to participate in politics and decision-making at the community and national levels. While the graduates are still young, they get involved in community issues, from efforts to end violence against women and ensure the enforcement of the 30 percent quota for women's political participation, to promoting self-employment initiatives and other strategies to alleviate poverty.

"To me, they are future Kudirats," Hafsat says. "They are pioneering women in Nigeria's political life. I am working to ignite a flame in the hearts of a new generation of Nigerians that says, 'Nigeria can be good again. We can make it happen.'"

Hafsat describes what drives her with quiet confidence, resilience, and strength: "There is enough. We are enough. Those are the words I live by. There are enough resources for everyone and they will expand as they are shared. We are enough. We have the ability within us to solve all the problems that plague our world."

ANEL TOWNSEND DIEZ-CANSECO
Peru

"When the people overwhelmingly reelected me to Congress I took this not as a prize but as a challenge to continue to make their voices heard through the halls of government."

During the 1990s, Peru, like many Latin American countries, suffered from widespread corruption and organized crime. The economic implications of corruption—drug trafficking, labor exploitation, tax diversion, and illegal purchases in the defense sector—was calculated at nearly a billion dollars. Meanwhile, the quality of social programs and institutions such as hospitals and schools deteriorated. Fifty-four percent of Peruvians lived below the poverty line.[15]

During those years, the regime used intimidation tactics against its opponents. As a journalist working to expose corruption, Anel Townsend's phone calls were tapped, she was often followed, and threats were made against her son. At the time, it seemed there was no way forward. But politics are in Anel's blood. Her father was a well-respected politician who fought for increased government transparency. And in the early 1990s, as she was traveling throughout the country reporting stories of corruption and human rights abuses, she began to feel that she could no longer simply report on Peru's troubles—she needed to act to resolve them.

In 1995, Anel joined Javier Perez de Cuellar's presidential campaign against Peru's incumbent president Alberto Fujimori. A few months later, the party asked her to run as a parliamentary candidate. She knew she would have to commit to political and social change as never before. "I was aware it would be a constant battle to maintain a career fully committed to fighting against corruption as well as fighting against those who don't want to give political space to a woman," she said.

In Peru, polls showed that young people and women were disengaged and had no confidence in politicians. As a new leader, she wanted to earn back their trust and participation. Anel became one of the strongest voices for change. During one of Fujimori's speeches to Congress, which was televised to the nation, Anel, a new congresswoman, approached the president's podium and placed an empty pot in front of him. The audacity and symbolism of her gesture drew attention, as it represented both Fujimori's empty promises and the fact that Peruvians were starving.

In November 2000, engulfed in a corruption scandal and an outcry over human rights abuses carried out by his government, President Fujimori was impeached and removed from office. As Peru began to transition away from an autocracy that controlled business, the media, the judicial and legal systems, and at the same time a network of crime rings, Anel saw an opportunity to create a more transparent and decentralized government—a true democracy for Peru.

On my first trip to Peru in February 2003, I heard about the fierce young congresswoman who had won the highest number of votes of any member of Congress in the country. Anel was dedicated to combating corruption—working with her colleagues to expose the links between corruption and drug violence and to mandate that the government disclose budgets and other information for public oversight.

The U.S. embassy in Peru arranged a meeting for me with Anel in a small coffee shop in downtown Lima during that first visit. Speaking with great conviction, at a rapid-fire pace, Anel tells me that she has just been appointed minister of women's affairs. She plans to focus on building dialogue between the government and NGOs to foster transparency and new partnerships. On occasion she pauses, almost overcome with inspiration, or perhaps to catch her breath. She is a visionary and dreamer, but also equally focused and unrelenting in her cause. She tells me how she has already taken the initiative to draft new legislation to protect the rights of women at home and on the job and pushed it through Congress. In collaboration with local and international NGOs, she has been able to persuade the Constitutional Affairs Committee to add an amendment to the constitution that says the state must respect and promote gender equity in political participation.

Anel may have been one of only a few women legislators in her country's Congress, but she has not been afraid to champion women's equality. For her, equality is not about favoring one group over another. It is about helping her country as a whole. "Women are the backbone of our communities," she said. "For many years they did the work that the government was not doing—organizing community centers and educational programs, providing food to the hungry and healthcare to the sick. It seems only fitting that as government authority is decentralized, increasingly women are running for new local council and regional government positions."

In 2001, Anel worked to pass a law mandating a 30 percent quota for women on a party's candidate slate for Congress. Since then, more and more women have risen to positions of political leadership at both the local and national levels. She is confident that as more citizens—women and men alike—begin to take an active role in the political process, corruption in Peru will continue to decline and the economy will prosper. Anel has continued to promote gender equality and public transparency in Peru and Latin America, serving as an advisor to organizations such as the Inter-American Development Bank, the Inter-American Commission of Women of the Organization of American States, and the World Bank.

Anel can see that change is slowly making its way through Peru—and the region as a whole. She believes space for women's voices in politics is finally opening in Latin America, led by a few women who have defied the "givens" of traditional politics as she did. Michelle Bachelet, the former defense minister, was elected president of Chile in 2006; as the first female head of state in Latin America she blazed a new trail and transformed the region's vision of what power looked like. Dilma Rousseff became president of Brazil in 2011 and announced during her inaugural speech that she would fight for women's rights so that electing female leaders would become "a natural event." Since her election, an unprecedented wave of women have entered politics in Brazil in what has been dubbed the "Dilma Effect" by the media. Peru has yet to elevate a woman to the country's highest position, but each woman who stands up to lead in an ethical and transparent way, like Anel, brings that eventuality a little bit closer. Anel's driving force is, *Women will be the change; I will be their voice.*

SUNITHA KRISHNAN
India

"Amita was only three years old when her mother was tricked by traffickers. They promised that her daughter would have opportunity—a better life. Instead, they sold Amita. That's when her mother reached out, desperate to find her daughter. Together, we risked our lives. We confronted the traffickers, and rescued Amita. Thirteen years later, Amita is a teenager—an aspiring doctor. She is at the top of her class in school."

Sunitha Krishnan has devoted her life to breaking the violent cycle of sex trafficking, the slave trade, and the spread of HIV/AIDS in India. Standing just over four feet tall, she has taken on a monumental task as the founder of Prajwala—Eternal Flame—a nongovernmental organization that rescues children like Amita from brothels and helps them to rebuild their lives.

"Amita was inspiration, because even after her rescue, she remained vulnerable—there was nowhere for her to be safe, protected. Thirteen years ago, I decided that I would build a shelter," Sunitha recalled. "I built it for Amita."

Sunitha Krishnan's driving force was born of a trauma of her own: when she was fifteen years old, she was gang-raped by eight men. In the aftermath of the attack, Sunitha struggled to make sense of what had happened. She refused to see herself as a victim. Instead, she transformed her pain into fiery commitment, a vow to help end the sexual exploitation of women and children.

When I first met Sunitha, she told me that more than 90 percent of the children in her shelter are HIV-positive. I thought she meant that the virus had been passed from mother to child. "No," she explained. "All of the children in the shelter are survivors of sex trafficking. These are children who have been rescued from pornography, sex tourism, and prostitution. They are children who have been kidnapped, lured by false promises of employment, sold by their own parents, or trapped by debt bondage." At the time, the youngest child in the shelter was just three and a half years old.

Prajwala operates according to five pillars: prevention, rescue, rehabilitation, reintegration, and advocacy. Each pillar plays an integral role in a strategy Sunitha has developed with partners and staff over fifteen years.

First and foremost is prevention. To stop commercial sexual exploitation before it starts, Prajwala operates a network of eighteen primary schools in the state of Andhra Pradesh. The schools are open to children of women in prostitution and other kids who live in the neighborhoods surrounding the brothels. The goal is to equip these children with the skills and knowledge to choose a different life from what they see at home. The schools are a safe place for the kids to be during the day, which also keeps them out of the hands of brothel owners and traffickers. Sunitha leads community-based efforts in the slums, villages, schools, and colleges where her team works to identify and connect with at-risk women and children. They operate with the knowledge that prevention is far more effective than a cure.

The second pillar is rescue. Prajwala's rescue and recovery teams coordinate with the police to infiltrate unlawful brothels; as of December 2011, they had rescued more than 6,436 women and children. Several members of Prajwala's team are former sex workers who were themselves rescued. They aid police in sorting the victims from the perpetrators hiding in their midst, and are able to connect with the victims with genuine understanding and compassion.

Rehabilitation is slow work. Many of those rescued have been drugged to the point of addiction, brutalized, and brainwashed. Their ability to trust another human being is almost nonexistent, and recovery can be a long and painful process. In the care of social workers, medical staff, and peer counselors, victims slowly become survivors over time.

Many continue to live with HIV. They must overcome daunting physical, psychological, and economic challenges, and they face ongoing threats from traffickers and social stigmatization by the community.

Victims of trafficking are frequently ostracized by society. The reintegration process is the most challenging part of Sunitha's work. She developed Prajwala's economic recovery program, which offers sustainable and viable livelihood options and reintegration services. Hundreds of survivors receive training as welders, carpenters, masons, security guards, cab drivers, camera operators, and screen printers. Corporate partners provide additional training and job placements that pay wages well above the national average.

Advocacy is the fifth and final pillar. Sunitha and her team realize that their work alone will not be enough, so they collaborate closely with partners across sectors. She works with state authorities to shape antitrafficking policies that help survivors access rehabilitation services and financial restitution. In 2010, the state of Andhra Pradesh adopted a policy that she drafted, establishing minimum standards of care that shelters and service providers must meet.

"It has not been an easy road. I have had to pay a heavy price," she said. Trafficking in persons is a lucrative enterprise, and there are many who would like to silence Sunitha. She has been brutally attacked more than a dozen times because of her work. She receives death threats frequently. But she always shows up for work the next day because she wants to send a powerful message: "I am not a victim. They do not intimidate me. They cannot stop my efforts."

This commitment took shape years ago. "When I was violated I could have decided to see myself as a victim. That is the easy way out. I looked to others to pull me out of the darkness I felt, but they could not. I felt isolated and ashamed. I wondered if it was my fault. But then I looked inward." What she found was a wellspring of strength, her own personal fire.

"I see so much pain, so much suffering. Sometimes it is too much," she confessed. "But there is great power to be found in pain. I believe you must *harness the power in the pain*. That is the driving force of my life."

HAWA ABDI
Somalia

"If I stop working, the women will have nowhere to go. The women are essential to stability."

Since its founding in 1960, Somalia has been ravaged by war and scarred by decades of poverty and turmoil. Territorial disputes and clan conflicts have undermined any kind of centralized control over the country. The result is a patchwork of autonomous regions overseen by clans, who have each formed their own ruling governments. As a result of ongoing violence, much of the central government has been forced to operate outside of Somalia in the neighboring countries of Kenya and Djibouti.[16] While peaceful elections in 2009 provided some hope for progress, interclan hostilities and instability persist, along with pervasive poverty. And while there are virtually no official data, violence against women, rape, and domestic violence are known to be common practice.[17] UNICEF estimates that 98 percent of women have undergone female genital cutting (FGC), which often leads to serious health complications.[18]

In much of Somalia, health care is rudimentary at best. At a young age, Hawa Abdi witnessed her own mother die in childbirth, and she made a promise to herself to someday support Somali women's medical needs. At age seventeen she won a scholarship to study medicine in Ukraine. After being trained as an ob-gyn, Dr. Abdi returned to Somalia to work as one of the country's first female gynecologists.

At home in Somalia, Dr. Abdi got married, had three children, and worked in the government-run hospitals. Acutely aware of the consequences of famine and war on women and children, she sought then-President Mohammad Said Barre's permission to open a single-room clinic in Lower Shabelle, a village outside Mogadishu, to assist nomadic women in childbirth. In 1983, the clinic opened on her family's 980-acre farm. She was convinced that in order for the country to progress, there must be people on the ground promoting change.

In 1991, the Somali government collapsed, famine struck, and foreign aid groups fled the country out of fear of the emerging violence. Dr. Abdi stayed. Instead of pulling back her services, she expanded them. Her family farm turned into a hospital, school, and refugee camp, where 78,000 people found refuge and medical treatment for war injuries, severe malnutrition, and disease.

The once one-room clinic has since become the Hawa Abdi Hospital, where Dr. Abdi works with her two daughters, Amina and Deqo Mohamed. The hospital has three operating rooms, six doctors, forty-three nurses, four hundred beds, and an eight-hundred-student school and adult education center offering literacy and health classes for women. The education curriculum includes the discouragement of FGC. Her commitment is desperately needed: as of 2011, in a country of nearly ten million people, there were only 365 doctors.

At times, that commitment has meant risking her life. In May 2010, the camp was overrun by hundreds of Islamic militants, and Dr. Abdi was held hostage for a week. Rather than submit to her captors, she stood up and asked them, "What have *you* done for society?" Under pressure from the United Nations and other international supporters, the invaders finally gave up and left the village. Dr. Abdi immediately resumed her work.

Although we had been following her efforts for years, my first meeting with Dr. Abdi was in 2010, when Vital Voices joined *Glamour* magazine to honor her and her daughters with *Glamour*'s Women of the Year Award, for their tireless efforts to save and better the lives of women in Somalia. The partnership was in more than name: together Vital Voices and *Glamour* initiated a fund that directly benefits the Hawa Abdi Hospital. Following a 2011 article that Nick

Kristof wrote about Dr. Abdi in the *New York Times*, we raised close to $200,000 in a matter of days to help Dr. Abdi continue to provide refuge, medical attention, and education to approximately 78,000 Somalis in need.

Dr. Abdi is insistent that her camp is not just about serving urgent needs; it is about creating a new paradigm. A generation of boys growing up in the camp has been taught to respect women as their equals. They also serve on a security force to protect the camp. Domestic violence and FGC have been outlawed, and there is a jail on the property for men who engage in violence against women.

Dr. Abdi's driving force is *Finding hope in hopelessness*—and the belief that she has no choice but to lead.

CHAPTER TWO

STRONG ROOTS IN THE COMMUNITY

INTRODUCED BY DR. NGOZI OKONJO-IWEALA

Coordinating Minister of the Economy and Minister of Finance, Nigeria

WE ARE AT THE CUSP OF HISTORY. This is a defining moment for the developing world and especially for its women. I have always believed that we can take charge of our own destinies if we have the courage to demand and lead change.

Throughout my life, I have felt privileged to contribute to the endeavor of development. In the process, I have met women who have a formidable will to fight for the progress of their communities; their fight is ongoing, and in many countries, it is being won. These visionaries, leaders, young and old alike, derive their strength from the realization that progress is born from within; reform begins only after you understand the character of your community, its unique challenges and potential to overcome them.

I have committed much of my life to serving the development of my country and my continent because I believe that the story of Africa's success is ours to determine. I have seen what happens when unrealized potential meets opportunity and a people and nation come together to claim the future. Each woman in this chapter shares that abiding conviction in the possibility of her country and its people—Lubna Al-Kazi has it for Kuwait, Maria Pacheco for Guatemala, Mu Sochua for Cambodia, Roshaneh Zafar for Pakistan, Kah Walla for Cameroon, Rosana Schaack for Liberia, and Adimaimalaga Tafuna'i for Samoa.

The force of my determination is buoyed by my strong sense of belonging to a community of women in my village, my country and the world over. In my work, I have viewed serving my country and serving our international community as mutually reinforcing acts, with mutually beneficial aims—they are one and the same. Change that starts at the local level, as the stories of these leaders show, echoes far beyond. It is my conviction that if one leads effectively and improves the condition of their community—their street, their neighborhood, their town, their country—they contribute to the betterment of our collective community, our world.

This moment of our shared story calls for boldness and resolve to raise the stakes in our communities. When we lead from within, when we listen and adapt, our leadership evolves—it becomes transformative, it survives us.

I n 2000, the World Health Organization declared the water contamination crisis in Bangladesh the "largest mass poisoning of a population in history."[1] Water wells built a decade earlier to address the rise of waterborne diseases were discovered to contain toxic levels of arsenic in nearly half the nation's water supply. The international development community launched a multimillion dollar effort to respond to the crisis. After testing wells, they developed a communications campaign to alert communities to the dangers of drinking tainted water, and a plan to mark for an illiterate population which wells were safe to drink from. It couldn't have been simpler: safe wells were painted green; contaminated wells were painted red.[2]

This seemingly commonsense solution had unintended and disastrous consequences. Those who lived in villages with red wells were stigmatized. The same villagers who had been poisoned by arsenic were also unable to get jobs. Young women in "red well" villages were unable to find husbands, and there was a sharp rise in prostitution and trafficking of those women as a result. Taking matters into their own hands, many villagers repainted the red wells green, which in turn triggered a drastic increase in the rate of poisoning.[3]

Not only had the international donor community's solution failed; it had actually made the problem worse.

• • •

The Bangladesh water crisis is just one example of the consequences of "solving" a problem from the outside without the benefits of local insights. At Vital Voices, we believe that

41

the best way to promote positive and sustainable change in any community is from within. Since 1997, Vital Voices has invested in women leaders who promote change locally in their own communities, countries, and regions. We listen to and learn from the needs the women in our network express, and try to ensure that our work to promote peace and prosperity is consistent with their own efforts and goals.

This approach grew out of the organization's early history and Hillary Clinton's leadership after the Beijing women's conference. The advocates who attended the conference heard the First Lady's speech as a call to action and returned to their homelands inspired to make a difference. Mrs. Clinton responded by reaching out to women leaders, inviting them to share their concerns, and looking for opportunities to support their efforts. She understood that in the simple act of listening, she could help bring credibility to their causes. Between 1993 and 2001, Hillary Clinton visited more than eighty countries, primarily in the developing world, where women's voices were frequently unwelcome and unheard.[4] Her aim was not to propose her own solutions, but rather to learn from women who were working in the trenches, to amplify their voices, and to leverage her position to support their work.

Back in the United States, in collaboration with her chief of staff, Melanne Verveer, and the secretary of health and human services, Donna Shalala, Mrs. Clinton and her husband established the President's Interagency Council on Women in 1995. The council's mandate was to bring together the most senior women representing each federal agency, catalog what the U.S. government was doing to support women, and develop a plan to work across agencies to implement the Beijing Platform for Action. The platform had identified twelve critical areas of concern for improving the lives of women, from health to education to economic development.

In the fall of 1995, I returned from Beijing inspired by the women leaders I had met and desperate to share with my generation the knowledge I had gained about global women's issues. Still in college, I hosted a forum for hundreds of young men and women at my university, Emerson College, in Boston in March 1996. One of the invited speakers was the charismatic Theresa Loar, director of the President's Interagency Council. Stunned by the large turnout and interest of young people, she quickly recruited me to take an internship after graduation that year. I took another leap of faith and followed my passion for global women's issues to Washington, D.C., where I staffed this powerful and unprecedented White House council under the direction of Theresa and the associate director, Kathy Hendrix. One of the first things I saw when I walked into the office was a huge photograph of Mrs. Clinton at a podium. I recognized it instantly as from that life-changing conference in Beijing. Today, it still hangs over the desk in my office at Vital Voices.

In 1996, Madeleine Albright made history when President Clinton appointed her the first female U.S. secretary of state. That same year, Theresa Loar was appointed as senior coordinator for international women's issues, and I followed her and Kathy from the White House to the State Department to staff this important work. The day we opened the office, the Taliban moved into Kabul and said that women couldn't go to work and girls couldn't go to school. Our first task was to draft an official statement proclaiming that the U.S. government would not recognize the Taliban or condone their treatment of women. Such a clear statement about the value of women in society might not have been possible without a clear mandate from the top.

I vividly remember the excitement around First Lady Hillary Clinton's visit to the State Department in March 1997 to join Secretary Albright for an event to commemorate International Women's Day. Secretary Albright boldly stated that "investing in women is not just the right thing to do, it's the smart thing to do." This became a call to action, and Mrs. Clinton and Secretary Albright emerged as a dynamic "tag team" on global women's issues. Secretary Albright would raise issues in bilateral meetings with world leaders, and the First Lady served as an effective, albeit unofficial, ambassador for women, chairing roundtable discussions with women leaders and visiting microcredit cooperatives and shelters for women fleeing violence around the globe. This was a radical shift for the United States. For the first time in history, the American government committed to making the advancement of women around the world a top foreign policy objective.

Vital Voices was initially meant to be a one-time gathering that signified this new diplomatic commitment. Ambassador Swanee Hunt, who represented the United States in Austria, brought together women from Central and Eastern Europe and the former Soviet bloc countries, like Marina from Chapter One, to connect on the issues they faced in the early days of their new democracies. Mrs. Clinton traveled to Vienna to meet with the women leaders gathered, and gave the keynote closing address at the conference. Once again, she amplified the voices and concerns of women who were not heard. The shift to democracy across the region was giving rise to the feminization of poverty and a marked decrease in political representation. The opening of country borders had sparked a multibillion dollar enterprise of human trafficking, an issue that had gained little international recognition to that point. At the conference, a group of Ukrainian grandmothers and a young human rights activist, Oksana Horbunova, approached Melanne Verveer, who is herself of Ukrainian decent. They told her about a growing problem: the girls in their communities were disappearing. With diminishing employment opportunities and a loss of social benefits, many girls had been lured into taking jobs in neighboring, wealthier nations as nannies or dancers, only to find themselves forced into prostitution. This encounter fueled Melanne's steadfast commitment as one of our government's leading advocates to combat human trafficking; a few years later, the U.S. government passed the Victims of Trafficking and Violence Protection Act to provide tools and resources that address the growing scourge both domestically and abroad.

At that first Vital Voices conference in Vienna, Secretary Albright made her commitment to advancing women clear to those at the State Department, the U.S. embassies in the region, and government leaders and members of the media. "As we approach the new century, we know that we cannot build the kind of future we want without the contributions of women. And we know that, in this region and around the world, women will only be able to contribute to our full potential if we have equal access, equal rights, equal protection, and a fair chance at the levers of economic and political power." American embassy representatives throughout the region who had nominated women leaders from their host countries to participate in the gathering returned home with a new commitment to carry these issues forward. As a result, millions of dollars of U.S. government resources were committed to advancing women as a critical means to achieving peace, security, and prosperity across the region.

Following that conference, our tiny office at the State Department was flooded with calls from women all over the globe who wanted us to organize a Vital Voices gathering in their region too. Without realizing it, we had created an opportunity for women to have their voices heard and their concerns taken seriously on the world stage. Vital Voices conferences gave women a platform to raise global awareness and financial support. Foreign policy leaders were now realizing that if half the population did not have access to education, economic opportunities, and equal protection under the law, then democracy, stability, and economic prosperity could not take hold. Policy makers were for the first time making investing in women's progress a strategic, proactive intervention. By the time I left the State Department in 2000, dozens of reporting cables were coming in each day from U.S. embassies, highlighting women's issues around the world; whereas when I began, there had been months before even one cable was received. This was a clear sign that the efforts of Secretary Albright, Mrs. Clinton, Melanne, Theresa, Kathy, Anita Botti, the deputy director of the office, and others would live on beyond their government tenure. This was sustainable change.

• • •

Perhaps most important, Vital Voices was a catalyst—a space where leaders came together across countries, cultures, sectors, and generations and, in meeting one another, were transformed. In the course of two or three days together, many of the participants began to self-identify as leaders for the first time, and that shift in thinking became critical to their success and ours. Through our work, we met women who understood the problems facing their communities and weren't cynical about solutions. They believed in their societies' potential. These women also possessed common strengths that have become integral to Vital Voices' understanding of women's leadership; strengths including the ability to develop strong roots in their communities, to empathize with others who live there, and to lead laterally, from within.

Over fifteen years, Vital Voices has identified this engaged, participatory approach as a common thread among the diverse women leaders in our global network. In fact, a body of independent research supports the view that women are more inclined than men to adopt participatory leadership styles.[5] Additionally, according to a study by the Inter-Parliamentary Union, nearly twice as many women as men enter political leadership positions through civil society and nongovernmental or community organizations.[6] A majority of the women we met first became interested in public policy through an issue that personally affected their lives, and pursued public leadership to address that issue. In essence, they sought power to change a reality they had lived.

Since 1997, Vital Voices has observed a trend among leaders who subscribe to participatory or lateral leadership styles. In our experience, those who lead from within root their aspirations in the community and seek power to empower others. They are most successful when they are able to stay grounded in the needs of their communities, even as they gain greater exposure themselves, and to ensure that they are responding to their communities' interests, and bringing other people along.

For example, Marina Pisklakova's direct relationship to women living with domestic violence catalyzed her development as a leader. As she continued her work to combat gender violence, she leveraged her growing influence as a platform to expand her services and to promote greater awareness of the issue, so that the community's own commitment to stamping out violence would grow as well. Marina measured her success not by her personal achievement or international recognition, but by her community's progress.

Those who lead from within and have strong roots in the community, like Marina, maintain a close proximity to and keep strong lines of communication with the individuals they direct, serve, or represent. Unlike the well-meaning outsiders who imposed a solution to the Bangladesh water crisis, participatory leaders steep themselves in local knowledge. They understand the complexities involved in promoting positive change and can quickly identify and respond to changes on the ground. In Bangladesh, such a leader would have been better positioned to recognize and address the rise in prostitution and trafficking across affected villages.

Furthermore, because participatory leaders are a part of their communities, they are often more committed to transparency and accountability. Participatory leadership relies on collaborative decision-making processes and community buy-in. As such, participatory leaders collaborate with others, first to define a strategy for change and then to monitor the implementation of that strategy. Community members can see their leaders' efforts and hold them accountable for achieving stated goals. Successful participatory leaders understand that they must mobilize necessary stakeholders and solicit the support and guidance of those who will be affected by their strategy. Engaging the community from the outset fosters a sense of community responsibility, where community members are equally dedicated to ensuring the leader's success at promoting change. Reforms driven this way have the potential to be more sustainable and democratic in nature than solutions that are imposed top-down. At Vital Voices, we have seen that this participatory style gives women a leadership advantage.

When asked why women tend to adopt inclusive leadership styles, international women leaders from our network consistently cite the qualities of empathy and emotional intelligence, which stem from social and cultural gender paradigms that encourage these qualities in women. As mothers, aunts, sisters, and daughters, women have long been validated and praised for their ability to understand, appreciate, and identify with those around them. Indeed, these qualities, traditionally thought of as "soft" qualities, have helped women achieve decision-making power and influence in the home and have a significant role to play in helping them advance in the public sphere. Groundbreaking research by Daniel Goleman, who brought forth the concept of "emotional intelligence," found that exceptional leaders demonstrate a high degree of self-awareness, self-regulation, motivation, empathy, and social skills.[7]

Despite the benefits that come with participatory leadership, leading from within poses considerable challenges to women's leadership development and the overall effort to legitimize women's leadership in mainstream society. In contrast to the centralized, highly public power of traditional leaders, in the participatory or "lateral" model leaders share decision-making authority and are positioned within a community of collective power. Those who lead from within, including participatory women leaders, are harder to distinguish as leaders.

In fact, many of the women who worked with Vital Voices in its early years did not even consider themselves leaders, despite their significant accomplishments. For this reason, Vital Voices promotes an enabling environment for women's leadership and highlights the ways in which that leadership is different from traditional, more masculine models. The more that women recognize and appreciate their own leadership potential, the more opportunities they will have to spark meaningful progress for everyone.

LUBNA AL-KAZI
Kuwait

"We were always told, 'Be patient. Women will have their political rights when the time is right.' Forty years later, here in Kuwait, our time has finally come."

Kuwaiti women are among the most educated women in the Arab world, making up nearly 70 percent of the country's university students;[8] they are senior engineers, leading doctors, and prominent academics. Yet until 2005, they did not have the right to vote or stand for political office.

When Kuwait gained its independence in 1961, Sheikh Abdullah Al-Salem Al-Sabah, the progressive Kuwaiti ruler at the time, developed a constitution that proclaimed all people as equal. But in that day, that really meant all men. As Kuwait began to modernize, the emir believed change would happen naturally; that gradually, women would become educated and serve in parliament. But hope for progress was overshadowed by tradition, and women did not gain those rights.

By the 1970s, more women than men were attending universities in Kuwait and abroad. Dr. Lubna Al-Kazi was one of them, and when she returned to Kuwait she became a professor of sociology at Kuwait University, where she organized with other women in the community and spoke out. They felt the time had come for them to have a say in the political affairs of their country. Although they organized numerous public campaigns, they were not taken seriously until the 1980s, when after much persistence they were finally allowed to meet with the ruler and members of parliament. After they presented their case for women's suffrage, one leader smiled and said, "I agree, yes, you should have your rights, and you will when the time is right." Lubna responded in frustration: "What will it take to prove that the time has come for women to be included? If women need to be educated, women are already educated. If you don't have a problem with us working alongside our male colleagues to strengthen Kuwait's economy and civil society, why would you have a problem with women working to strengthen our government?"

Ironically, it was war that started to change prevailing attitudes. When Saddam Hussein invaded Kuwait in 1990, women were full participants in the resistance. The emir, Sheikh Jaber Al-Ahmad Al-Sabah, and his government fled to Saudi Arabia, where they set up a government-in-exile. There, Sheikh Jaber declared that women would be granted their full rights as citizens of Kuwait after the war. When the war ended in 1991, women attempted to hold those leaders to their promise. Parliament was reestablished the following year, and women's suffrage was put to a vote. Once again, legislators decided women were not yet ready. Their reason? Women had no political experience.

Then in 1999, Sheikh Jaber made history, issuing a decree that women should be able to vote and stand for elected office. Inconceivably, the measure was voted down by two votes in the parliament,[9] but Sheikh Jaber's unwavering support of women's enfranchisement fueled Lubna's commitment to persevere. I met Lubna that same year during a trip to Washington, D.C. At the time, she was leading Kuwaiti Women's Social and Cultural Society, the premier women's rights group in Kuwait. She sought our support to train women to advocate for their political rights.

She and other women leaders realized that they needed to build a constituency of support to compel the government to act. Aware that some MPs shared their view that women should gain political rights, they set up meetings and invited them to join as allies. They also organized debates to educate the public and gain press attention and even engaged the wives of MPs and conservative leaders.

Lubna and her allies needed to prove to the Kuwaiti public that denying half the population their basic rights as citizens was legally, socially, and politically wrong. To do so, she knew she would have to dispel misconceptions among both men and women, such as the idea that political rights were sought only by elite, middle-aged women. She knew that many women themselves didn't see a need to gain political rights. Drawing on a lifetime of local understanding, Lubna and other advocates launched a petition, getting signatures of support from university students, businesspeople, parliamentarians, and even religious leaders whom she persuaded that suffrage was not a religious issue. They published the signatures in newspapers to demonstrate the diversity of support for suffrage.

International influence and events beyond Kuwait's borders also helped. In 2002, for example, women in Bahrain gained political rights a few months before national elections, but so close to the elections that they had little time to get organized. Not a single female Bahraini candidate was able to mount a winning campaign. Kuwaiti women were determined to be better prepared than their Bahraini counterparts. They traveled to the United States for political skills trainings organized by Vital Voices and other organizations. We also brought them together with female parliamentarians of other Arab nations to gain support and insights.

According to Lubna, "The tipping point came in 2001, when we saw time running out before the next election. We decided to shift the language from 'women's rights' to 'a strong future for Kuwait'—convincing people that our country's future should not be hijacked and decided by a few elites." This shift in the language of their advocacy efforts helped to engage young people, who began organizing public rallies. One of my favorite images from those days is a photo of young men and women marching together in matching blue shirts that read, "Women are Kuwaiti too." Blue represents women's suffrage. These young men who stood up for women's full participation helped to send the message that universal suffrage would be a benefit to all Kuwaitis, not just women.

Small factions within the government joined the lobby for women's rights. Dr. Rasha Al-Sabah, under-secretary of higher education and one of the emir's most trusted advisors, became a strong supporter for the cause. At one of the early Vital Voices conferences, she told Mrs. Clinton, "In Kuwait we don't want a skim milk democracy. We want a full cream democracy."

"When we finally did gain our political rights through a parliamentary vote in May 2005, it was a really euphoric moment," Lubna recalls. "It was not a decree that came down from the ruler; it was achieved through a truly democratic process. Word spread like wildfire. Within thirty minutes, all of Kuwait knew that women had their political rights at last."

A few months later, I traveled to Kuwait for the first time. Although Vital Voices had supported and trained Kuwaiti women, we had been careful to avoid the perception that American women were behind the suffrage campaign. The women in Kuwait taught us the power of drawing on local knowledge to drive positive change. We offered connections and ideas, but it was their knowledge of Kuwaiti society that informed and fueled their advocacy. A strategy imported from outside the country never would have been able to generate the massive shift that led to success. Lubna believes that if you educate women about their rights, they will use them: "This is what we have been doing by reaching women in different parts of Kuwait, showing them the rights the constitution has given them. Women of Kuwait now have the opportunity and responsibility to be engaged and informed citizens, not onlookers."

MARIA PACHECO
Guatemala

"The most difficult thing after war is not to rebuild the infrastructure, but to rebuild the hearts and minds of the people, to give them faith again in humanity. This is not something that can be found outside our country. It must be developed within our people."

For the first thirty years of Maria Pacheco's life, her country, Guatemala, was embroiled in a civil war that initially erupted between left-wing guerilla groups and government military forces.[10] By the time a peace treaty was signed in 1996, thirty-six years after the war started, over 200,000 people had been killed and more than a million people had been displaced.[11]

Maria grew up in a privileged community in Guatemala City at a time when there was a growing divide between those in rural communities who endured the brunt of the violence, and those in cities who for the most part were sheltered from the conflict. More than 90 percent of human rights atrocities during the war were perpetrated by state forces, and 83 percent of victims were Mayan people fighting for economic and social justice, including increased land rights.[12] Years after the conflict ended, violence and intimidation persisted throughout the country. Organized crime syndicates operated with relative impunity. Distrust permeated relationships between Mayans and non-Mayans.

In 1993, tired of the increasing violence in Guatemala City, Maria moved her family to the mountains. A biologist by training, she became an organic farmer. When nearby villagers learned of Maria's expertise, they asked her to help them make their parched fields more productive. Maria discovered that the land was barren. The area was suffering from drought and famine, and the collapse of the coffee market left entire villages without income.

The indigenous people were desperate for a way to provide for their families. On the day I met Maria, she told me a story about a Chortí Mayan woman named Doña Santa whose child was sick with fever. When Maria asked her why she didn't take him to the doctor, Doña Santa told her, "I have five dollars. With this money I can try to save this child or I can feed my other seven children for a month."

Maria could not accept a reality for her country in which a mother had to choose which of her children would live or die. So she embarked on a mission to bring opportunity, prosperity, and most important, dignity to communities that others had long forgotten. She understood that a solution could not be brought in from the outside. "My people don't want charity," she said. "They want partnership. They have skills. They have a rich heritage. They can develop products. They just need support, investment, and access to markets to sell these products."

Guatemala is home to twenty-two different ethnic groups, each with a unique culture and traditions. To honor these traditions and to open the door for women to earn an income, Maria created Kiej de los Bosques (Friend of the Forest), which initially worked with indigenous women's groups to connect their local artisanal products to national and international markets. "The Mayans believe that the *kiej*, the deer, is the protector of the *bosques*, the forests. That is what we are trying to do, to protect our most cherished cultural traditions while providing opportunities."

The goal wasn't just immediate relief from hunger. It was to improve the quality of life, rehabilitate indigenous communities, and preserve an ancient culture. For Maria, it was also about long-term reclamation of the area's land and water resources through reforestation and conservation. Families were taught to develop irrigated organic gardens in order to improve their nutrition. Through Kiej, quality of life for families in local communities improved dramatically, and Maria's work drew national attention. Then the First Lady of Guatemala challenged Maria to bring her outreach to thousands more.

In 2006, around the same time as the First Lady's request, Vital Voices first encountered Maria. She had been selected by the U.S. embassy in Guatemala City to be among the first group of mentees to participate in the Fortune / State Department Global Mentoring Partnership, the brainchild of Dina Powell, then–assistant secretary of state, and Pattie Sellers, senior editor at *Fortune* and chair of the Fortune Most Powerful Women's Summit. The program, coordinated by Vital Voices, pairs emerging entrepreneurs from around the world with top Fortune 500 women executives for a month-long mentoring experience, which many mentees have called transformational. Maria's mentor was Kathy Calvin, CEO of the United Nations Foundation and former AOL executive.

"From the minute I met Maria, I knew this was going to be a two-way street," recalls Calvin. "She had so much energy and passion. I saw a woman who had her entire country in her back pocket." Throughout the mentorship, Maria carried around a little notebook in which she had written a quote from Henry David Thoreau: "Go confidently in the direction of your dreams, live the life you have imagined." Maria believes very strongly in creating the world she envisions. She took what she had picked up during her mentorship and returned to Guatemala to expand the work of Kiej, to accept the First Lady's challenge, and to bring prosperity to more communities.

Kiej de los Bosques quickly evolved into a company that designs and exports products made by rural women's groups based on their skills following global fashion trends. As of 2011 these products were exported to over fifteen countries under the umbrella brand Wakami (www.wakamiusa.com). Working with Vital Voices trainer and entrepreneur Karin Shipman, Maria collaborated with her partners and the people of one community to successfully launch Maya Botanika, a textile product line employing rural Guatemalan artisan women. The increased income has allowed families to send their children to school, and for the first time in many communities, a generation of students has the option of attending university.

Recognition of Maria's work spread. In 2007 Vital Voices honored her with one of our Global Leadership Awards for Economic Empowerment. The First Lady of Guatemala, Wendy de Berger, traveled to Washington, D.C., to join Dina Powell in presenting Maria with the award. In 2008 USAID awarded Maria and a group of Guatemalan colleagues a grant to launch an innovative mentoring program in Central America that aims to connect young women to skilled mentors throughout the region.

But it seems Maria was just getting started. She recognized that there are indigenous communities all over the world who are struggling with issues similar to the Mayan communities in Guatemala. Just a few months after she returned home, Maria teamed up with her mentor, Kathy Calvin, and the United Nations Foundation to launch a pilot program replicating methods she honed in Guatemala at a

World Heritage Site in Mexico. The goal of the program is to simultaneously protect the environment, traditions, and local culture while developing sustainable sources of income for the indigenous population. If it is successful, Maria sees the possibility of a global model in which local groups will be mentored and supported as they design their own ways to protect unique natural resources, cherished traditions, and the livelihoods of the people who uphold them.

MU SOCHUA
Cambodia

"When a child says, 'Give me back my soul,' I translate it into 'Give me justice.'"

In 1972, when Mu Sochua was seventeen years old, her parents put her on a plane from Cambodia to Paris to save her from the massacres of the Khmer Rouge. She never saw them again.

Between 1975 and 1979 a struggle against Communist forces left nearly half the population of Cambodia, roughly three million people, dead.[13] Many of the country's most educated citizens were executed. Thousands more died of starvation and hardship in internment camps. Following the 1991 Paris Peace Accords and with support from the United Nations and the international community, Cambodia has seemingly grown into a fledgling democracy, perhaps even a success story. But as Sochua discovered when she returned to Cambodia after eighteen years away, a harsh reality lay just beneath the surface.

Sochua had taken a long and winding path back to her homeland. Moving from Paris to San Francisco, she tried to build a life for herself and became a community leader among Cambodians living in the Bay Area. Still, night after night she dreamt of returning to her country to find her family.

In 1989 Sochua finally made her way back to Southeast Asia, working on the Thai/Cambodian border in a refugee camp. "When I first arrived, I searched every face, trying to locate my parents." In 1990 she returned to Cambodia and found a country transformed. The people were living in poverty; the beautiful countryside she remembered was riddled with land mines; and Phnom Penh had become a haven for sexual deviants preying on vulnerable young women and girls. She talked to local women and became consumed by their gruesome stories of sexual violence and abuse. Their voices became fuel for her fight.

Sochua quickly became a leading voice in the women's movement in Cambodia, working with women's networks and human rights organizations to promote peace and to include strong provisions in the 1993 constitution to protect the human rights of women. In 1995 she attended the United Nations Fourth World Conference on Women in Beijing. It was there, after hearing Hillary Clinton intone "women's rights are human rights, and human rights are women's rights," that she decided to run for public office to give women a greater voice.

I met Sochua on my first visit to Cambodia. By that time she had gained an international reputation as Cambodia's first *female* minister of women's affairs. The irony was lost on no one. Sochua was a renegade within the cabinet, pushing for change within her own government. She was a minister by day, but at night she walked the red-light district in Phnom Penh, listening to women's stories. One of her first acts as minister was to negotiate an agreement with Thailand allowing Cambodian women trafficked as sex workers to return to their home country in lieu of being jailed. She drafted and defended the Domestic Violence Law in Parliament. She then pioneered the use of frank television commercials and toured the country for five years to spread the word about trafficking to vulnerable young girls and boys.

She definitely ruffled a few feathers in a government focused on promoting Cambodia's successes to the outside world. During my first visit, she told me, "If I want to use this position to make change, I have to be willing to risk everything. There is a saying in my country: 'Men are gold, but a woman is just a piece of a white cloth.' If the gold gets dirty, it can be wiped clean, but a white cloth, once it is stained, it remains that way forever. We must change this."

Sochua knew it would take more than her lone voice to change societal norms. As minister, she promoted a new saying: "Men are gold, but women are precious gems." Within a few years, she developed and launched an innovative campaign to bring about women's wider participation in public life. She worked with civil society to encourage women at the grass roots to become candidates for *commune*, or local elections, the first of their kind in the history of Cambodia. In 2002, 25,000 women ran for public office as candidates; 2,250 of these candidates, roughly 9 percent, won seats.[14]

For her work against sex trafficking of women in Cambodia and neighboring Thailand, Sochua was conominated for the 2005 Nobel Peace Prize. But not everyone praised her efforts. Cambodia is one of the most corrupt countries in the world, and many were getting rich off the buying and selling of innocence. By the time I returned to Cambodia in January 2005, Sochua had been ousted from her position as minister of women's affairs. I remember sitting with her in a restaurant in downtown Phnom Penh. A few nights earlier, a local antitrafficking organization had raided a brothel and rescued dozens of girls. The organization's shelter was then overrun by traffickers, working closely with local police, to "reclaim their property." Sochua believed you could trace the trail of corruption straight to the top.

It would be easy to feel powerless and frustrated by the seemingly unassailable abuse of power, but Sochua's spirit and commitment did not waver. She left the ruling party and went on to win a seat in Parliament as an opposition candidate. A year later she was the first woman to become secretary-general of a political party in Cambodia. As one of the opposition's top leaders, she faces constant threats and intimidation from those in power, yet Sochua remains steadfast in calling for international attention to government corruption and human rights abuses overlooked by her government.

In my seven trips to Cambodia over nine years, the trafficking problem has seemed to only get worse. In the wake of the global economic crisis of 2008, thousands of garment workers lost their jobs, which has meant shrinking economic opportunities for women. It's a vicious cycle. "Women are hit hardest in this downturn," Sochua explained, "and a whole new population will become vulnerable to traffickers."

In Cambodia the voices of those in power are easily heard, whereas it is far more difficult to find space for those who feel wronged. Sochua is working to create a pipeline of local women leaders in Cambodia who will one day compete at the national level. At the same time, she advocates for a 30 percent reservation of parliamentary seats for women candidates. "Having joined the opposition party, my focus has been strongly on democracy and human rights." She also advises a wide network of civil society groups and trade unions on strategies to widen space for democracy.

One of Sochua's most successful strategies has been to join forces with various groups, at either local, national, regional, or international levels. She focuses on long-term development, which includes cultivating human capital in a country where most of the teachers, doctors, and judges were executed years ago by the Khmer Rouge, considered the most lethal regime of the twentieth century.

Sochua believes government must develop and implement policies that create special measures and opportunities for women so that they can reap a proportionate share of Cambodia's development. Discrimination and violence against women can only be addressed when society as a whole values women as human beings and as equal partners.

Sochua spends nearly 80 percent of her time walking the campaign trail and meeting with her constituency. I asked her once why she does this when she is so well known and loved by her people. There is no question that she will win elections. "I do it because I want to know them," Sochua responds without hesitation. "I need to know firsthand what it feels like to lose a child to disease or malnourishment or human trafficking. I want to understand what a family goes through when their property is seized by the government. The only way that I can represent my people is to know what it is like to walk in their shoes. I do not know any other way to lead."

ROSHANEH ZAFAR
Pakistan

"That's the role that I've always seen myself play—a bridge. I am comfortable in a community with my clients and staff in any part of Pakistan, and I am equally confident speaking to the presidents of the world."

For many working in the development sector, poverty reduction is the steepest of uphill climbs. For some it begins to seem unassailable. Roshaneh Zafar, an economist at the World Bank office in Islamabad, was frustrated by the development community's inability to make rapid progress to improve the lives of the world's most impoverished families. Discouraged and searching for a better solution, she found herself at a conference in 1992. There she met Dr. Muhammad Yunus and became fascinated with his pathbreaking work in microcredit. Founder of the now famous Grameen Bank and winner of the 2004 Nobel Peace Prize, Dr. Yunus had shown that when small loans were given to women with no collateral, not only did the women improve their lives economically, but it turned out that their loan repayment rate was *significantly* higher than traditional banking models.

"I was a complete stranger," recalls Roshaneh, describing her introduction to Dr. Yunus, "but he was so mentoring, so open. He has an allure of calm and understated confidence about him that makes you want to follow him anywhere. He invited me to come to Bangladesh and to observe his model. It was impossible to turn down such an offer." So she accepted.

In 1994 she traveled to Bangladesh and worked closely with the Grameen Bank to learn how microcredit was transforming the lives of the poorest of the poor. After a year had passed, she asked how she could continue to be of service. Yunus told her that Grameen could carry on in Bangladesh. Where she was most needed was back home in Pakistan. He gave her $10,000 in seed capital and told her to start her own program. In 1996 Roshaneh returned to Pakistan and began her work.

She knew it wouldn't be easy to bring microcredit to women in Pakistan. Since gaining independence in 1947, the country has struggled to develop economically and politically. A woman's role in Pakistan remains largely restricted to the home. At 36 percent, literacy among women is more than 20 percent lower than that of men.[15] In addition, Pakistan's cultural practices and banking regulations were different from what she had seen in Bangladesh. But Roshaneh was determined to help. In 1996 she founded the Kashf Foundation with the motto "Microcredit for women, by women." Charged with the mission of both job creation and economic empowerment for women, the Kashf Foundation gave microcredit loans to women and employed only women tellers in its branches.

Though I had been following Roshaneh's work for years, she and I first met in 2009 through one of our partners,

Amanda Ellis, who was leading cutting-edge work at the World Bank to measure and report on the power of harnessing women's economic potential. What impressed me most was Roshaneh's self-awareness as a leader. Entrenched in the communities in which she serves, she listens to the local women and leads with their interests at the forefront. This groundedness and humility have enabled her to recognize and learn from her mistakes—and ultimately, to be a more successful leader as a result.

For example, in launching the Kashf Foundation, Roshaneh encountered a series of challenges. In contrast to the seemingly unqualified success of the Grameen Bank, her borrowers defaulted on their loans at a far higher percentage. In the first two years, she found that 20 percent of Kashf's loans were stuck. She was an economist by training and an expert in international development. She had worked side by side with Muhammad Yunus in Bangladesh, but somehow the Grameen model that had thrived in Bangladesh was not working as she had intended in Pakistan.

To understand what had gone wrong, Roshaneh and her team went directly to the women they were trying to help. "Our premise was that we had to work with women only and not involve families," Roshaneh explains. "But the first two years (1996 to 1998), when some women were unable to pay their loans and we tried to involve the men in their families, they were not forthcoming. They said they had not been consulted in the first place." She began to see the problem.

Despite the best of intentions, the Kashf Foundation had marginalized some women borrowers by not enrolling the men in their lives as stakeholders. Because they had not been engaged in the decision, some men resented their wives. Roshaneh realized that in order to empower women, she needed to empower everyone. "We revised our strategy and looked at microfinance *through* women to support the economic needs of *families*, for we realized poverty affects all members of a household, however in different ways. We therefore needed to have a multipronged approach."

While remaining true to her mission of empowerment for women, by women, Roshaneh changed her approach. She made it policy to include men in the lending process, and to hire men to make the enterprise more inclusive. She spent almost eight years implementing the changes necessary to make the model work, but ultimately, she was tremendously successful. Over fifteen years, the Kashf Foundation has dispersed over $225 million through more than 1.2 million loans and continues to provide training, financial literacy, and employment for poor Pakistani women.

As a leader, Roshaneh was willing to make changes based on what the community needed. She understood the context in which she was working, and she adapted her tactics and adjusted her priorities in order to be more effective. Her flexibility allowed for the creation of a new and successful model of microcredit. And now Roshaneh can confidently advocate on behalf of the women she serves. She is living her driving force, *Helping women transform themselves and transform society.* She knows what works, and she is carrying their stories across the globe.

KAH WALLA
Cameroon

"I believe in people's innate ability to succeed. I believe that success is defined by ourselves and is within each and every one of us. The job of a leader or a facilitator or a politician is to help people define success for themselves, identify the ways in which they can succeed, what they need to do to succeed, and to accompany them along the road to that success."

Cameroon is a central African country of vast wealth, but that wealth is concentrated in the hands of a powerful few.[16] By contrast 40 percent of the population live on less than a dollar a day, and half of the country lacks electricity or clean water.[17] Since independence in 1960, presidential power has been passed only once. There have been periodic elections, but Cameroonians have come to accept that those elections will be marred by corruption and fraud.

In Douala, Cameroon, Kah Walla owns and runs Strategies!, a management consulting firm. The business fulfills one of Kah's life missions. She wanted to create a woman-led model of African success that could compete anywhere. With Fortune 500 clients on five continents, she's done just that.

Raised in a family of strong women, Kah felt that she needed to understand people in order to fight for them. After completing her studies in the United States, she returned home to help make her country a better place. She wanted to work on behalf of those who did not have a voice; those who did not have access to the advantages she had enjoyed.

A lifelong activist, Kah eventually decided to run for city council in Douala. "I moved from activism to politics because I realized that no matter what you did as an activist, you would come up against the system . . . it was difficult for me to imagine myself in the political arena. But at the same time I was really uncomfortable at each election. I felt like, *Kah, you can't keep complaining about this and saying how awful it is and not acting.*"

At the local level, politics gave Kah an opportunity to build direct relationships with constituents. She listened to members of the community every day and used her position to empower them as members of civil society. Kah worked across party lines to empower women to take on leadership roles, and encouraged women in her community to do the same.

I first met Kah in South Africa in February 2008 at a training program that Vital Voices had organized for African women lawyers and entrepreneurs. During the program, participants created advocacy projects designed to remove legal barriers to women's economic progress in their home countries. Across the continent, women faced common financial barriers like lack of property rights and access to capital. These inequities made it impossible for African women in business to compete on a level playing field. Kah's charisma, authenticity, and passion for helping others develop and implement bold ideas are infectious. A natural leader, she worked alongside other women across Africa to define barriers in their communities and to create tangible plans for positive movement.

As a local city councilor, Kah had noticed that the nine hundred women working in the Marché Sandaga, one of the largest produce markets in central Africa, had no voice in how the market was run. Male traders, who made up a small fraction of the market, held thirty-nine out of forty-one positions in the market's governing association. With support and a small grant from Vital Voices and the Bill & Melinda Gates Foundation, Kah organized advocacy training for the market women, informing them of their rights and helping them establish their own association to advocate for better working conditions. As a result, the women successfully fought double-taxation and improved working conditions throughout the market. Kah gave these women a platform to be heard and encouraged them to speak out for themselves.

"As women—and I think as African women—we have a tendency to go to the table sort of begging, sort of saying, 'Please, I'm in a really bad situation, could you please help me out, please do something about this, it's really awful.' And what I've learned is, we need to flip it around completely," Kah explained. "We are a significant part of these economies. And if this economy wants to grow—if this country wants to grow—then it's a good idea that we sit at a table and that we start talking to each other and seeing what's best on both sides. In that way we can pass legislation which is favorable to us as women, but which is also very good for the country."

Kah quickly learned that when women entrepreneurs received training in basic business management, their revenues increased. Investing in women had immediate and substantial impact. But she also found that the system created barriers to carrying out some of the opportunities she set out to create. For example, if the women entrepreneurs had access to more capital, their businesses could soar. But as women they struggled to get loans.

"I realized you have to shift the entire system," Kah told me. "You have to make it such that there are more resources at the base level. When people are making the decisions at the grassroots level, at the level where it affects their lives, there will be a definite shift in power."

In 2011 Kah announced her candidacy for president of Cameroon. In the fifty years since its independence, Cameroon has had only two presidents. She immediately faced intimidation and threats. At a demonstration in support of electoral reform to ensure that the voice of every citizen would be heard, she was forced to stand on a traffic median and bear the full force of a water cannon aimed at her by police.

Then, on May 20, 2011, Cameroon's National Day, she was at the Mont Febe Hotel in the capital city of Yaoundé when four men intercepted her near the elevator and forced her into their car. Identifying themselves as police, they seized her cellular phone and luggage and searched her belongings. She repeatedly asked to be released until finally, hours later, they dropped her off outside her home in Douala and drove away.

Kah refused to be intimidated. She fought on, but again, the 2011 election was marred by irregularities. Despite the disappointment, Kah was unfazed. And she had been noticed: the Cameroon media voted her Best New Politician after the elections.

Kah knows that even though she didn't win, she made a positive impact through her campaign. "I think I've been able to bring home to certain people, especially women and young people, but I think men in the Cameroonian society as well, that we can do this. We can do it differently. We can do it with very high standards, and we can do it on the issues that are about us. We can address these problems."

For Kah the answers to society's issues lie with the people who make up that society. Her leadership style reflects this completely. When she talks about the touchstone of her beliefs, it is always very simply, "I believe in people."

ROSANA SCHAACK
Liberia

"Being able to go through the process of suffering—not having basic things—it put me in a state that I could identify with people that I work with . . . really have empathy for what they go through. . . . At my standard of education and exposure I am able to reach up . . . it is possible for us to join forces with the different sectors so that our fight can be conquered."

As a child, Rosana Schaack benefited from the love of two families from drastically different backgrounds. Born into an indigenous Bassa family living in Liberia, local doctors diagnosed Rosana with polio at just two years of age. Unable to meet Rosana's health needs, her family offered her up for adoption to an American missionary family living in Liberia's capital city of Monrovia. Adopted at the age of six, Rosana enjoyed both the nurture of her biological family and the love of her adoptive family. Today Rosana points to her upbringing as one of the most formative experiences shaping her leadership ambitions and abilities. It reinforced her love of country and afforded her the ability to navigate difference and diversity. Yet the importance of this experience was not always apparent to Rosana. It took a series of events transpiring throughout the course of Liberia's civil wars to bring the power of this experience to light.

In 1989 conflict erupted in Liberia, giving way to two civil wars lasting fourteen years. Looking back, Rosana recalls her feelings of shock: "We never knew that . . . the horrific things we were going to see could have ever been imaginable. We had seen things on TV . . . but it never occurred that it could have happened to us." As violence increased, expatriates were forced to evacuate the country, including Rosana's adopted parents. In her early thirties and a mother to three young children, Rosana had no choice but to stay. She had never become an American citizen. So Rosana remained in Monrovia with her children to endure Liberia's civil conflict.

As they moved about, trying to stay out of the line of fire, the family faced constant violence and at times crippling hunger. In the summer of 1990, fighting in the capital forced her to leave her American parents' home and walk thirteen miles to her own home on the outskirts of Monrovia. The walk took Rosana and her family two days. They had to pass through multiple checkpoints and endure numerous obstacles. Along the way, Rosana recalls: "I found myself the leader of this little group of displaced people, thirty-three people! I didn't want my kids to see fear in me. I had to be strong for them and for the rest of the group I was leading"—and she remembers coming into her own. Looking back on this time, she recalls: "I had a strong sense of purpose; for me, life was not just giving up. I'm not a person that gives up easily."

In 1994 Dr. Shana Swiss recruited Rosana and five of her peers to develop a survey, conduct field research, and facilitate discussions to learn about the challenges war imposed on Liberian women and girls. This experience marked the beginning of Rosana's work on violence against women, and exposed her to the unique challenges faced by girl soldiers, which has become integral to her work today. A nurse by training, with access to resources and firsthand knowledge of the difficulties of war, Rosana recognized that she had a powerful platform to aid in her country's healing process.

As the second civil war came to a close in 2003, Rosana established the nonprofit organization Touching Humanity in Need of Kindness (THINK Inc.) to engage in the peace-building process. THINK envisions a nation with transformed communities, where the marginalized and poor, especially women and children, are protected, healthy, educated, and self-sufficient. Since 2003 Rosana and her team at THINK have worked tirelessly to empower women and children in Liberia. When the international community came in to deal with the aftermath of war and the deep scars that remained, there was a tremendous emphasis on programs for boy soldiers. Overlooked by the international community, girl soldiers were incredibly vulnerable; they required highly nuanced and customized rehabilitation services. Recognizing the severe emotional trauma these young women had faced, Rosana and her team designed an innovative nine-month empowerment program to help reintegrate into society the girls who had fought or served as sexual slaves for warlords. She believes that just as it takes nine months to create a life, it also takes that long to begin to heal and rebuild a life.

When designing her organization's strategy, Rosana set out to build bridges between clients and her staff. She recognized that every individual has a unique perspective and has been affected by conflict differently. When the war was over, Liberians were angry at the former combatants who perpetrated crimes against humanity. Even though the former girl soldiers Rosana worked with had been victims themselves, there was a tremendous amount of stigma around them. As Rosana built her team at THINK, she promoted tolerance and reminded counselors and practitioners that they must separate their own trauma from their work and forgo judgment of their clients. Trust, security, transparency, and accountability emerged as core values for the organization.

Rosana attributes much of her professional success to her experience living as a refugee and internally displaced person during Liberia's civil wars. She believes that she is able to identify and empathize with the community she serves as a native Liberian who experienced the devastation of war. Rosana understands that her prestigious education as well as her privileged upbringing allowed her to ensure the success and sustainability of her organization. With a unique ability to identify and navigate diversity, Rosana brings a spirit of connecting and collaborating to her work with THINK. In fact Rosana joined the Vital Voices / AVON Global Partnership to End Violence Against Women in 2010 to connect and collaborate with human rights leaders in South Africa, the Democratic Republic of the Congo, and around the world. As such Rosana and her team at THINK are working to share challenges and best practices with practitioners across Africa, to effectively improve their services at home.

Rosana's experience in civil war helped to define her vision and act strategically, with clarity and strength of purpose. Her education, understanding, and empathy towards the community she serves helped her to advance her mission. Most notably, Rosana's exposure to various communities helped her to think big. She used her platform as an educated professional to establish a thriving organization that empowers the vulnerable and underserved. Along with her sensitivity and foresight, Rosana's local knowledge has enabled her to be successful in her efforts to rebuild her country through investments in women and girls.

ADIMAIMALAGA TAFUNA'I
Samoa

"We try to find opportunities so that women and their families are able to earn an income where they live for their daily needs."

Like many small island nations in the Asia Pacific region, Samoa is often overlooked by the rest of the world. Yet the island nation and its neighbors are rich with natural resources and boast some of the most beautiful landscapes in the world. Its culture is robust, characterized by strong Christian traditions and a focus on extended familial clans. However, for the people of Samoa and the greater Pacific region, economic opportunities are scarce; violence against women is pervasive; and women's political participation ranks among the worst in the world. According to 2009 estimates, Samoa's growth of GDP is valued at negative 5 percent;[18] 46 percent of women experience abuse from intimate partners;[19] and women hold only 8.2 percent of parliamentary seats.[20] While the statistics paint a bleak picture, leaders like Adimaimalaga ("Adi") Tafuna'i see a bright future for Samoa and the Asia Pacific region, one that is rooted in indigenous values.

Adi has dedicated her life to service, working to empower women and underserved rural communities. She began her career in 1991, when she co-founded Women in Business Development Inc. (WIBDI). Originally, Adi established this nonprofit organization to convene business professionals who sought to advance the economic status of women in Samoa. Yet shortly after the organization's founding, natural disaster hit the country. Back-to-back cyclones descended, and a fungal blight decimated the country's taro root crop, Samoa's staple food and main export product. Responding to changing conditions on the ground, Adi and her co-founders recognized an overwhelming need by those who lived in rural villages, and they shifted the focus of the organization to meet this need. Reflecting on this period, Adi explained that "people who were living in rural Samoa were suffering a lot more than we were. So we decided to work there with them."

Stifled by a lack of economic opportunity in their home communities, many young Samoan villagers move to urban centers or emigrate to Australia, New Zealand, and the United States in search of livelihoods. Finding employment far from home, these young people send money to their families, effectively creating cash economies in rural villages. With remittances flowing into these communities, rural villagers are deterred from generating their own income locally, and young workers are isolated from their family clan. This causes a tremendous strain on Samoa's economy and culture. Adi understood that this unique challenge required new and innovative solutions: "you don't find people starving in the Pacific . . . you have to look at poverty in a different sense; there's definitely a poverty of opportunity. People need cash, but they don't have the opportunities to make that cash where they live, and I think that's so important."

To ameliorate the lack of economic opportunity in Samoa and the greater Pacific, the international community recommended the implementation of microfinance programming. Replicating successful models from Southeast Asia, the United Nations Development Program brought microfinance into Samoa in the 1990s. However, the Pacific is extremely different from Southeast Asia, and the microfinance model that helped millions thrive in that part of the world was less successful in Samoa. Women were given loans to build businesses without an understanding that there were no markets for their products. So Adi set out to find a new strategy that would work within the realities of the region. She looked for ways to keep families together, reduce dependence on remittances, and spark local business. To do so, Adi turned to one of Samoa's natural resources—virgin coconut oil—which because of its health and beauty applications held value on the international market. In 1995 Adi and WIBDI launched an initiative to employ rural Samoans in virgin coconut oil production by placing oil presses in rural villages and training families in coconut oil production. She also approached international health and beauty companies to create a market for this product. A major breakthrough came when Adi brokered a partnership with The Body Shop, effectively opening up a market that would employ hundreds of Samoan families in coconut oil production.

Recognizing the importance of local knowledge, WIBDI implemented a model of programming that encouraged weekly face-to-face contact between its staff and coconut oil producers. Responding to the social emphasis placed on Samoan family culture, the organization further tailored its programming to serve families as opposed to whole village communities or individuals alone. Over time Adi and her partners have identified this approach as key to the organization's success: "we found that when a family was earning cash for themselves, they tended to take more responsibility for the project, stick to it longer, and put more money back into it." In addition, Adi and her partners have seen a ripple effect from their work. As client families begin to generate income, they pass their earnings on to the community through churches and schools. As the demand for coconut oil has grown, WIBDI has been able to export its programming and share the market with other communities throughout the Pacific region.

I first met Adi in Vanuatu, when she participated in the Emerging Pacific Women Leaders Program, a joint project between the AID programs of New Zealand and Australia, the World Bank, the U.S. State Department, Asian Development Bank, and Vital Voices to foster leadership and economic opportunities among women in twelve Pacific Island nations. Despite her unassuming leadership style, women from across the region speak of her as if she were a rock star. As of January 2012, Adi has enabled more than 1,500 families to gain economic opportunities to support themselves, effectively strengthening Samoa's economy and offering its youth an alternative to emigration. Leading collaboratively, with local knowledge and love of country, Adimaimalaga Tafuna'i is helping to transform individuals' lives and create a different future for Samoa and the greater Pacific region.

CHAPTER THREE

AN ABILITY TO CONNECT ACROSS LINES THAT DIVIDE

INTRODUCED BY SENATOR KAY BAILEY HUTCHISON

Honorary Co-Chair, Vital Voices

THE HISTORY OF AMERICAN WOMEN IS ONE of resilience, unflagging optimism, and perhaps most important, willingness to collaborate in the face of adversity.

The courage to stand firm on matters of principle is one of the hallmarks of leadership. But in both public service and business, I've often found the only way to break through tough problems and produce lasting change is to engage with people with whom you sometimes disagree.

In the U.S. Senate, I have been fortunate to work with and develop personal rapport with many fine people on both sides of the aisle. In this context, my friendship with former Senator and now Secretary of State Hillary Clinton has been and continues to be exceptional.

We bonded soon after she came to the Senate in 2000. We weren't the most likely legislative allies: one of us a Republican from Texas and the other a Democrat from New York. We were on opposite sides of many issues. But we found several shared goals to help women and families, and formed a successful partnership on this common commitment. We worked together to produce major legislative progress in education and in family-friendly tax policy. And in 2001, I was honored to join Secretary Clinton at Vital Voices as an honorary co-chair of the board, embracing the concept of partnerships on a global scale.

When I was first elected to the Senate in 1993, there were seven women senators. Today there are seventeen. There will be more of us in years to come. We have grown to be a bipartisan presence in Congress—not because we agree on every issue, but because we are willing to reach out in order to find the ways and means of making our country better.

Alyse writes in this chapter that "a true leader understands that she cannot make change alone. After all, leadership is measured by an individual's power and ability to guide *others*." That's where collaboration arises. For many women, leadership has involved pushing past obstacles. But this certainly has not been done alone. In my experience in the Senate, you look for places where you can find agreement, and build on where your values overlap in order to create a true and lasting partnership.

My female colleagues in Congress have demonstrated time and again that they are strong leaders—their work together has made a real impact on society.

As evidenced by the women featured in this chapter—Inez McCormack, Asha Hagi Elmi, Noha Khatieb, Latifa Jbabdi, Oda Gasinzigwa, Rita Chaikin, and Afnan Al Zayani—women leaders come from countries all over the world, and collaboration is the common thread and the reason for the significant progress for their communities.

On August 10, 1976, during some of the darkest days of the "troubles" in Northern Ireland, a vehicle of the Provisional Irish Republican Army swerved onto the sidewalk in Belfast, killing three young children who were walking with their mother. The accident occurred when British troops fired on the vehicle, certain that they had seen a rifle pointed at them from inside. The driver was shot and lost control.

In the days that followed, there was more focus on whose side was at fault in the incident than on the tragic loss of three young lives. Betty Williams, a Protestant who lived in the neighborhood and had witnessed the tragedy, had had enough of what she called the "sickening cycle of useless violence."[1] She began gathering signatures on a petition for peace, and she reached out to the maternal aunt of the dead children, Mairead Corrigan, a Catholic.

Together Mairead and Betty represented many women whose frustration had come to a head. "We are for life and creation, and we are against war and destruction," Betty declared, "and in our rage in that terrible week, we screamed that the violence had to stop."[2] Mairead and Betty organized peaceful protests and rallies, rapidly igniting a movement across the country and demonstrating that it was still possible to transcend the conflict by working together for reconciliation. That same year Mairead Corrigan and Betty Williams were awarded the Nobel Peace Prize for crossing the lines that divided their society. Egil Aarvik, vice chairman of the Norwegian Nobel Committee, said at the Nobel award ceremony: "Betty Williams and Mairead

Corrigan have shown us what ordinary people can do to promote the cause of peace. They have taught us that the peace for which we strive is something that has to be won within and through the individual human being."[3]

Twenty-two years later, after two generations of women had navigated and negotiated complicated grassroots politics, continuing to build a constituency for peace, the White House hosted leaders from Ireland and Northern Ireland who were engaged in the peace talks that ultimately led to the Good Friday Agreement. It was March 1998, and Mrs. Clinton had traveled to Northern Ireland in the previous year. She was well acquainted with the challenges women endured. That day in the White House, the First Lady met with two women, a Protestant social worker and a Catholic academic, Pearl Sager and Monica McWilliams. Pearl and Monica had come to speak with Mrs. Clinton about the next stage of empowering women as agents of peace.

In February 1996, nearly three decades since the start of the "Troubles," the British and Irish governments had announced the establishment of All Party Talks to decide Northern Ireland's future. Participation in the talks would be determined by elections. The seven political parties put forth their representatives. Pearl and Monica—along with women community leaders across the country—were stunned to see that not a single woman had been included. Not having women at the negotiating table meant accepting a settlement and a future that women would have no meaningful role in shaping. That was unacceptable. After all, it was women who had been in the trenches, slowly and methodically weaving the fabric of society together and creating an infrastructure within communities to support a peace process. Indeed the problem they faced is not unique to Northern Ireland: between 1992 and 2010 only one in thirteen participants in peace negotiations worldwide was a woman.[4]

Pearl, Monica, and a group of women representing all ages, religions, socioeconomic backgrounds, and political affiliations across Northern Ireland decided to take matters into their own hands. Within a few months, they had launched a new political party, the Northern Ireland Women's Coalition (NIWC). The NIWC was made up of women from diverse political parties and religious backgrounds, united behind a common cause: creating a more peaceful and prosperous future for Northern Ireland and making sure that women had a voice in shaping it. Monica and Pearl knew that banding together as women might be their only chance of being heard, but they also knew they had a compelling advantage over other parties. Together they stood as a flesh-and-blood example of the Northern Ireland they hoped to create: one of mutual tolerance and respect, where bridging differences led to lasting change.

When the Good Friday Agreement was finally signed by all parties, at 5:19 P.M. on April 10, 1998, it was clear to Pearl and Monica that women, with their influence on families and communities, would be critical to implementing the peace accord. Even with an official voice at the table, Pearl and Monica had been marginalized and even ridiculed in the process. They had come to the White House to ask Mrs. Clinton to champion their cause. Monica and Pearl knew the important role she could play in raising the profile of the work of women leaders. Shortly after the meeting, it was decided that the second Vital Voices conference would be held in Belfast, Northern Ireland, to bring women leaders together from across the region and unite them around the critical role they would play in building the future.

In contrast to our experience with the first Vital Voices conference, which had focused on Eastern Europe and the former Soviet Union, there was little U.S. government funding available to support a conference aimed at bringing together women from Northern Ireland, and even less for follow-up projects. It quickly became clear that in order to make a lasting impact, we would need to engage the private sector.

In 1998 Vital Voices became the first U.S. government, public-private partnership to benefit women globally. Businesswomen like Judith McHale, then-CEO of Discovery Communications, and Mary Daley Yerrick, a public relations executive and entrepreneur, as well as Donna Cochran McLarty, an advocate for women and children, and Marylouise Oates, author and activist, were among the first to step up to support Vital Voices from outside of government, committing private sector resources and pro bono talent to further our efforts. Corporations and foundations brought needed financial and in-kind support.

What had been born out of funding necessity soon developed into a highly effective model, not only for increasing support but also for heightening awareness among corporate and private sector leaders of the value of women's leadership around the world. The public-private model was critical, as subsequent Vital Voices conferences were held in Latin America, the Baltics, and Central Asia, and global initiatives brought women together from the Middle East, Africa, and Asia.

In addition to working with the private sector, we engaged regional bureaus at the State Department and other U.S. government agencies. We also reached out to and formed strategic partnerships with government leaders around the world and international institutions like the World Bank, the Inter-American Development Bank, and the United Nations. American embassies throughout the globe collaborated with host country governments to identify and support emerging women leaders as participants. Perhaps subconsciously, we were modeling the connecting and collaborating behavior of women leaders we had encountered in Northern Ireland and in so many other parts of the world.

• • •

The previous chapter explored how the power of local knowledge and being rooted in the community enables leaders to promote positive, sustainable change; that when a leader is deeply connected to her community, she acquires a nuanced understanding of the system and society she hopes to affect. This understanding serves as a foundation for the third common thread or behavior we have witnessed in successful leaders: an ability to connect, collaborate, and *cross lines that divide*.

Women leaders around the world who have embraced the concept of leading with local knowledge understand the dynamics between varied stakeholders and make a concerted effort to anticipate the effects of their actions in context.

Joseph Nye, former U.S. assistant secretary of defense and Harvard professor, stated that "modern leaders must be able to use networks, to collaborate, and to encourage participation." He highlighted how "women's non-hierarchical style and relational skills fit a leadership need in the new world of knowledge-based organizations and groups that men, on average, are less well prepared to meet."[5]

Studies show that women tend to consider all the options and connections prior to making a decision or completing a task, while men are primarily focused on the task itself.[6] Vital Voices mentor and one of the founders of Oxygen media, Geraldine Laybourne, has often said, "We [women] are not just multi-taskers, we are multi-thinkers."

We have seen that locally rooted women leaders make connections deliberately, recognizing that they cannot create transformative change on their own. After all, leadership is measured by an individual's power and ability to guide *others*. Leadership is a relationship, and part of being an effective leader means connecting and collaborating with stakeholders who can support one's efforts, not only to launch positive change but also to carry it forward. The most effective women leaders cultivate relationships with individuals, organizations, and institutions that will be affected by their vision for change. Especially noteworthy is the fact that these relationships are not limited to those who already support the leader's aspirations. A leader's relationships have to reach *all* the people who have a stake in change—whether they perceive themselves as gaining or losing from the process.

Building such relationships requires honesty, integrity, flexibility, humility, transparency, and the ability to reframe one's vision and strategy into a win-win scenario, so that everyone can be vested in its success. Empathy is an extraordinary asset in this regard, as it enables leaders to identify, relate to, and respond to other people's hopes and fears. Women tend to have a strong ability to empathize and are often characterized as having a high EQ (emotional intelligence).[7]

Frankly, the experience of women as a marginalized population also gives them a unique advantage. Women have a deep desire to be heard, seen, and understood, and they recognize that need in others. In so many places in the world, "being heard" is a daily struggle. Women leaders who have experienced this tend to be more aware and accepting of all stakeholders, within and without traditional structures of power.

As a leader develops a network, she engages individuals, organizations, and institutions in open dialogue, soliciting honest, open feedback and demonstrating the willingness to rework her strategy to maximize feasibility and fairness for everyone involved. Additionally, as the leader builds a wider network of support, she looks for ways to create partnerships. The women whom Vital Voices has worked with tend to be more inclusive in their leadership styles, because they know firsthand how it feels to be excluded from decision-making and denied access to power.

Studies also suggest that women tend towards "transformational" leadership.[8] This means that women view their professional aspirations and responsibilities in terms of getting others to transform their self-interest into the interest of the group by focusing on a goal. Research has shown that women's transformational leadership style motivates others to look beyond their own individual interests and focus on the good of the group.[9] As a leader embraces the knowledge, expertise, and ability of those in her network, she generates goodwill in the community or organization in which she works; and as members of her network invest their time and energy in a relationship with the leader, they become invested in seeing her succeed. Claudia Lago, a leader we work with in Brazil, explained this leadership style: "Women are always looking at who's in the room and how to effectively engage all their skills and abilities. We think laterally."

At Vital Voices we have learned that this kind of lateral thinking is essential in motivating others to your cause. The only way to catalyze lasting change is to collaboratively engage those people with whom you disagree, who come from different backgrounds, hold different beliefs, and have different agendas. We have watched the leaders we work with acquire unlikely allies who have informed their strategies, raised the profile of their work, and in some cases played a pivotal role in implementing the strategy. We have tried to incorporate this valuable lesson into our own practices as we seek to connect and facilitate partnerships across boundaries of geography, culture, and belief.

Take, for example, the issue of human trafficking, which as a global issue has gained traction and visibility in a relatively short amount of time. Back in 1997, when Ukrainian women approached Melanne, desperate to find a solution to the growing disappearance of young women in their country, the issue was for the most part not recognized by governments or the public. Most people had no idea that modern-day slavery existed around the world, even in the United States. Although there is still a long way to go, many countries now have laws on the books, and the issue is commonly highlighted in the media. This progress is the direct result of a vastly diverse coalition of people around the world who have stepped forward to bring attention to and eradicate the practice. In the United States, Republicans and Democrats have reached across the aisle to coauthor legislation, and multiple federal agencies and international institutions are now sharing information. Luis CdeBaca, U.S. ambassador to combat human trafficking, has said: "Partnership is critical. Laws are on the books and governments are beginning to partner with civil society to ensure that law enforcement and criminal justice officials understand the complexities of trafficking and are trained to identify and protect victims." In addition, the private sector is collaborating with countries around the world to develop codes of conduct and to trace the supply chain. Faith leaders are lending their moral authority to create a culture that demands justice. Oksana Horbunova, the Ukrainian antitrafficking activist who first approached Melanne, has said, "the traffickers have powerful global networks, so we are building our own, working with new and sometimes unlikely partners."

Working so closely with women from many countries and cultures, we know there is far more that unites us than divides us. Women find commonalities and opportunities to bond—over our children, our careers, our challenges, and our hopes—even when we come from vastly different backgrounds or perspectives; this is something I have seen in action time and again, going back to my Eritrean and Ethiopian roommates in Huairou, China.

By 2000 Vital Voices had hosted five major international conferences and scores of follow-up training programs reaching more than three thousand women leaders from government, civil society, and business. We had increased the resources allocated to support women throughout the U.S. government, but perhaps most important, we had raised the profile of women's issues. Those who had started as naysayers had begun to see the value of investing in women as more than just social policy. It was truly a successful foreign policy.

But the Vital Voices Democracy Initiative, based out of a little office in the State Department, was outgrowing its U.S. government roots. Women from around the world were returning home and establishing their own Vital Voices chapters. Women in Haiti wanted to be connected to women in South Africa, and women in Kuwait wanted to gain advice from women in Argentina. The leaders wanted a website to post photos and messages to each other, even though at that time few U.S. government agencies had their own websites.

In February 2000 we held a strategic retreat just outside Washington to ask twenty-five of the most actively involved women leaders how we could best support their efforts going forward. It was the first time we had brought them together globally, and the gathering was awe-inspiring. Women from places as diverse as Russia, Nigeria, and Cambodia shared how their association with Vital Voices had given them strength and power; and how much it meant to know that they were part of something larger than their own struggles, something that connected them to women around the world.

The leaders we convened felt that Vital Voices had the potential to become a global movement. But to do so, they believed it had to become an independent entity, giving the organization the freedom to partner across all sectors of society. We agreed. Our experience in Northern Ireland and other places around the world also made it clear we would need to more proactively engage private sector support to bolster financial support for this work. McKinsey & Company, a leading management consulting firm that had been involved with Vital Voices conferences, provided a team of global, pro bono consultants over the next two years to transition the organization from a U.S. government initiative to a nongovernmental, nonprofit organization.

Even though Vital Voices was initially developed as an initiative of the Clinton administration with the strong leadership of Hillary Clinton and Madeleine Albright, the organization has always brought women together across political lines in the United States as well as around the world. Mary Daley Yerrick, a successful Republican entrepreneur, attended the first Vital Voices conference in Vienna, Austria, to train and mentor emerging entrepreneurs, and she has been involved ever since. She and a prominent Democrat and advocate, Donna Cochran McLarty, who had actively participated in Vital Voices' efforts in Latin America, worked side by side as co–vice chairs of our board to register Vital Voices as a nonprofit and to set up its new offices in July 2000.

Melanne Verveer left the White House in January 2001 to build Vital Voices as a nonprofit, nongovernment organization and served as the chair of the board for the next eight years, and later as the CEO. Without her vision, energy, and commitment over all those years, Vital Voices would not be where we are today. At the same time, Theresa Loar left the State Department and served as the organization's first president. When the time came to establish the name of our new nonprofit, we wanted to communicate the values of connecting and collaborating. We moved on from the Vital Voices Democracy Initiative and became the Vital Voices Global Partnership.

As we were establishing the organization, Mrs. Clinton was just stepping into her new role as a U.S. senator representing the state of New York. In a perfect example of connecting, collaborating, and crossing lines that divide, she reached across the aisle and asked Kay Bailey Hutchison, the senior Republican senator from Texas, and former Republican senator Nancy Kassebaum Baker to join her as honorary co-chair of the new Vital Voices nonprofit. They each understood that Vital Voices would thrive only if we could work across the political lines that typically divide us in America—a collaboration that was still going strong as the organization celebrated its first decade. Since our founding days, Vital Voices has had a strong bipartisan board of directors, yet we have always seen ourselves as nonpartisan. The cause of economic development, good governance, and human rights is something that all of us can get behind, no matter our political affiliation.

During the early days of the Bush administration, following the 9/11 attacks, First Lady Laura Bush and later her chief of staff, Anita McBride, were some of the first to reach out to the burgeoning Vital Voices nonprofit to look at how we could work together to support Afghan women, who were emerging from the oppressive years of Taliban rule. One of our first projects was to collaborate around an effort to send Afghan women, particularly widows, back to work making school uniforms, which would help Afghan girls go back to school with pride after years of being confined to their homes. Mrs. Bush, working with women through the administration, helped to sustain a focus on women's issues, particularly in Afghanistan.

In 2009 Melanne Verveer and Mary Daley Yerrick handed the reins to our current board chair and vice chair, Susan Davis, a successful businesswoman, and Bobbie Greene McCarthy, who served as former First Lady Hillary Clinton's deputy chief of staff. Both Susan and Bobbie had been Vital Voices board members since our founding and were deeply vested in the organization's strategic growth as women's issues gained greater global traction.

Vital Voices has similarly sought out partnerships with like-minded organizations, recognizing that we alone cannot create the "tipping point" for women's progress. In collaboration with New York University (NYU), Booz and Company, leading nonprofit TechnoServe, the Paul E. Singer Family Foundation, and many business, NGO, and government leaders, we have developed La Pietra Coalition's Third Billion Campaign. The campaign, led by former Starbucks senior executive Sandra Taylor, is a bold commitment to enable a billion women around the world to more fully participate in the global economy. We have also partnered with NYU to develop a Vital Voices course and with Georgetown University and the University of Arkansas to develop practical training programs for emerging women leaders and entrepreneurs. And we have collaborated with the Economist Intelligence Unit, the governments of New Zealand and Australia, the La Pietra Coalition, and ExxonMobil to develop the Women's Economic Opportunity Index, which ranks countries throughout the world, measuring their progress in tapping the potential of women as a driver of economic growth.

We have seen the power of collaboration replicated throughout our network of emerging women leaders. Most recently, working with emerging women business leaders and assisting them in taking their vision for sustainable growth to scale, we began to observe that sustainable economic change rarely happens in a silo. In 2011 Vital Voices' partner organization, the Cameroon Businesswomen's Network (CBWN), teamed with Cameroon's chamber of commerce to create much-needed market opportunities for women who farm cassava, part of the roots and tubers product segment that accounts for almost half of all crop production in Cameroon. Through this $2 million multisector initiative, the chamber agreed to purchase raw cassava from CBWN-affiliated women farmers to supply the government's cassava processing plant in Douala. Working together, over 150 women farmers have joined the initiative, creating jobs for over three thousand temporary workers and over $4 million in additional revenue for women-led farms. More broadly, with 5 percent of revenues going to the CBWN, the association has also created an income stream for its Guarantee Fund and Investment Club, allowing more opportunities for other local businesswomen to access expansion capital, grow their businesses, and generate more jobs and household income for local families.

Dozens of Vital Voices-supported, public-private partnerships have produced programs that combine the best of government, civil society, and business alike. As serial entrepreneur Ashley Maddox, who helped to broker the Vital Voices / McKinsey & Company partnership, likes to remind me, "the unexpected guest at the dinner party produces the most interesting conversation," which is another way of saying that the more diverse and unusual the partners involved, the more innovative the outcome.

INEZ McCORMACK
Northern Ireland

"When you accord the same understanding of human rights to those with whom you find you disagree, you have the right to classify yourself as a human rights activist . . . you have to trust your own courage, trust your own humanity, and trust your own capacity to be more than you are."

Just weeks after Mrs. Clinton's meeting with Monica McWilliams and Pearl Sager in the spring of 1998, Theresa Loar and I headed for Northern Ireland, where we spent much of the next year talking to women across the country in preparation for the Vital Voices conference in Belfast.

One of the most extraordinary women we met in this process was Inez McCormack. Arguably one of the most influential civil rights leaders in Northern Ireland, she played a critical role in shaping the inclusive equality and human rights provisions in the 1998 Good Friday Agreement that curtailed decades of sectarian violence. Having served as the first female president of the Irish Congress of Trade Unions, she has since campaigned for implementation of these rights as key to an understanding of conflict resolution based on the practice of justice. Her work is contributing to a growing recognition that the ability to participate is integral to deepening democratic practice and to reconnecting economic growth and social progress at the global and the local levels.

Inez became active in the Northern Ireland civil rights movement in the late 1960s and then became a trade union and equality activist, campaigning to organize and revalue the contribution of "forgotten" workers, most of whom were women. As a social worker in the early 1970s, she supported women in disadvantaged communities, where she encountered strong women with children, no money, and a bloody civil war raging in their backyards. The two main political traditions—nationalist and unionist—literally did not sit in a room together, and only communicated through shouting, threats, and violence. Between 1969 and 1998, the conflict known as the "Troubles" took over 3,600 lives.[10]

Women began working in the early 1970s to build a community infrastructure to support peace. The only rule was that all groups from any background would be included and must be treated with respect, regardless of their opinions. Many years before the official Good Friday peace talks began, women were working within the community to shape inclusive dialogues on equality and human rights. No one had to reject their identity or allegiances in order to come together. Behavior in the room was dictated by manners and listening to one another, which laid the foundation for working together with common purpose. Yet despite their innate strength, these women lacked the leverage and the capacity to effect change. "Equality" in Northern Ireland was expressed in the 60s as the need for "one man, one vote."

A few women community leaders, including Inez, undertook a grassroots initiative, "Women Seen and Heard," to make audible the stories of women's lives, so that their needs could be shaped into rights. It was an extraordinary and diverse initiative, which brought together women within and across traditions. In each area organizers asked the question "Who is not visible; who isn't in the room?" and set themselves the task of answering that question. In doing so, they addressed and slowly transformed the sectarian divide. They mobilized women around issues that affected everyone, no matter which religious or ethnic community—issues like childcare, education, health care, and violence. The value of the initiative was strongly supported by the European commissioner, Monika Wulf-Mathies, First Lady Hillary Clinton, Ambassador Jean Kennedy Smith, and Mo Mowlam, Northern Ireland secretary of state.

This high-level support gave them credibility when together with the local human rights NGO they founded the Equality Coalition to bring together diverse groups in civil society, including those who faced discrimination based on religion, politics, gender, ethnic background, socioeconomic status, or disability. Striving to find a common purpose, they created a shared understanding of what causes pain in the "other." They understood that it was critical to link equality to the advancement of economic opportunity. Northern Ireland's economy had suffered greatly during the "Troubles." They wanted to show that violence and exclusion diminished possibilities for a prosperous future.

Despite all the work women had done within the community to build support for peace, the prenegotiation period for the Good Friday Agreement excluded female voices. The main focus of the talks were the new constitutional framework, a ceasefire, and the decommissioning of weapons. The Equality Coalition reached out to women and other excluded groups across Northern Ireland, working to get the language of equality and human rights for all people into the Good Friday Agreement. They convinced others to frame the agreement in such a way that, respect, and dialogue, and when the peace process began they served as a model for how diverse groups could work together.

Inez's civil society Equality Coalition worked with political parties, including the Northern Ireland Women's Coalition led by Pearl and Monica, to create a new human rights institution and rules that required the participation of affected groups at every stage of decision-making as a working definition of the promotion of equality. "Peace talks are often about making the various political parties happy and addressing their agendas, not about getting at the issues that create exclusion," Inez explained. "You've got to create an environment where people can put aside the party agenda and work together as people—believing they have an economic stake in the community, a social stake in the community." The Equality Coalition had thirty-nine separate meetings with senior civil servants and policy makers to get the simple language that they had won in the Good Friday Agreement translated into law with mechanisms to measure impact.

Inez believes that a hundred years from now, when Northern Ireland's history is written, women will be credited for playing a major role, not only in stopping the violence but also in shaping sustainable practices of peace building. "I've won many victories, and it's easy to claim the victory. The question is, does the victory translate into change for those who need it most? And that leads to the question 'Who is not at the table?' That is my driving force. It's not a question about being just or being morally right. It's asserting that this is the smart economics and smart democracy of tomorrow. There has to be an active process, a democratic process that creates opportunity for the most excluded."

ASHA HAGI ELMI
Somalia

"Somali women crossed a bridge and there is no turning back. We are full partners in the process . . . . For the first time ever in Somali history, Somali women were given their quota . . . I call that a total revolution."

Somalia has long been one of the most destitute and dangerous countries in the world. Ruled for decades by a military dictator, Major General Mohamed Siad Barre, the country's government collapsed when Siad Barre was ousted in 1991. Civil war ensued, and as of January 2012, Somali society continues to be ravaged by divisive interclan warfare, famine, and disease. Tens of thousands of Somali citizens have lost their lives to hunger and many more to violence. In this context women and girls have become increasingly vulnerable. And yet, with the strength and determination of Asha Hagi Elmi, women have made tremendous strides towards political representation and empowerment.

In Somalia clan structures are an important aspect of politics and daily life. It is a patrilineal society, in which an individual receives his or her cultural identity according to the heritage of his or her father. Marriage is often used to build an alliance between clans. Such was the case with Asha Hagi Elmi. Born in 1962 in the Galgaduud region of Somalia, Asha married a man outside her father's clan. Like many Somali women, Asha was no longer fully accepted by her birth clan nor her husband's. The division between her heritage and her marriage left her with dual allegiance, and when fighting erupted she found herself in a devastating position.

Asha saw that women were frequently the first victims of conflict: raped, tortured, widowed, and isolated by clan divisions, watching helplessly as their fathers and brothers fought their husbands and sons. Yet Asha also saw opportunity. "I felt that I didn't fully belong to any clan, because no one trusted me as a full member. This painful moment made me realize that war has nothing to offer women except for death, destruction, and devastation. And that is where my motivation to take the risk to work for peace has come from. Because many women experienced a loss of identity between two different, warring worlds, I found that I had to create a new and different place where these 'outsiders' could belong." Asha recognized that women could be a solution to the deep cultural stalemate fueling clan warfare. Because many women were not identified with *any* clan, Asha believed they could become the bridge connecting rivals.

And so, in 1992, in an effort to realize her vision of a united, peaceful, humane, and democratic Somalia, Asha began to organize and founded Save Somali Women and Children (SSWC), a nonprofit organization based in Mogadishu with a presence across the country. Determined that women be involved in peacekeeping negotiations, Asha worked with SSWC to advocate for the formal recognition of Somali women's individual identities and rights, a radical concept in Somalia. Then, seeing that the five national clans enjoyed a legitimacy that women collectively did not, Asha and her fellow activists formed the Sixth Clan, created exclusively for Somali women. The effort brought down a firestorm of criticism and death threats, but Asha stands by the idea. "Had it not been for that identity . . . Somali women would have never had a chance to be part and parcel of the Somali political process. So I turned to that identity and turned to that strategy, thinking outside of the box with the formation and creation of our identity as women."

The road was not an easy one, but Asha believed in her mission so strongly that she was willing to risk her life for the future of her country. "I know that one day I will be killed [but] I would rather die making a difference. I'm doing it for my daughters, for a new Somalia." Her efforts have paid off. The Sixth Clan was officially recognized in 2000, and Asha became the first woman to have a seat at peacekeeping negotiations during the Arta peace talks that same year. On August 29, 2004, Asha Hagi Elmi was selected to become a member of the Transitional Federal Parliament, Somalia's legislative body, which elects the president and prime minister and has the authority to propose and pass laws. For her efforts to build peace and bring women's voices to the fore, Asha won the Right Livelihood Award and became one of the Clinton Global Citizen Award recipients in 2009.

Though her nation remains desperately poor and unstable, Asha has seen progress. As of 2011 she stands among twenty-five women who serve in the national parliament; through her work as a legislator and as the chair of Save Somali Women and Children, she is shifting the social and political paradigms that have long ruled her homeland, and she is promoting women's political involvement, economic development, and education. The situation for Somalia remains dire, but Asha continues to be hopeful and action-oriented: "The Somali solution is very clear: we need a comprehensive political solution, and the proper vehicle for that is reconciliation—genuine, all-inclusive, and serious reconciliation—dialogue, [and] confidence building among the clans....We need all those positive, practical solutions." Through her work, Asha demonstrates each day that women are invaluable to the peace-building process.

NOHA KHATIEB
Israel

*"I think the magic happened when
I saw that the classroom was full of
Arabs and Jews and they could be
normal together and sit on the same
carpet and play together. I just had to
give them the support and the love
to understand and see each other."*

The conflict between Israelis and Palestinians is one of the world's most polarizing and seemingly intractable problems. Despite the committed efforts of influential leaders over the past half century, little progress has been made toward peace. Generations of Palestinians have grown up under occupation; and Israelis have grown up in fear of terrorists and rocket strikes.

Even as tensions between Israelis living in Israel and Palestinians living in Gaza and the West Bank make the headlines, 1.5 million Arabs live within Israel's borders, as Israeli citizens.[11] Sharing the same territory, these Arab Israelis and Jewish Israelis are separated by invisible lines that divide schools and communities. With little substantive contact and years of growing resentment, it is common for them to consider each other the enemy.

In 1998 Noha Khatieb, an Arab Israeli, heard that teachers were being interviewed for a new integrated primary school called Hand in Hand, a radical effort that had garnered a sliver of support among progressive Israelis. The model was based on the integrated schools that had successfully united communities in other countries, like Northern Ireland. Noha had an overwhelming feeling she had to be involved.

"I grew up as a Palestinian Arab in a Jewish city," she explains. "I grew up knowing the Jews, speaking the language, telling them that I am a Palestinian, that I am normal and human. My whole life was telling people that I have legitimacy. When I heard about this integrated school, I knew I would know how they felt. I thought, *I can help.*"

She insisted that she be given an interview, and when it was finished, she was offered a position. The night before her first day as a teacher, however, Noha started second-guessing herself. Should she speak Hebrew or Arabic? What if there was conflict? Would the experiment be an immediate disaster? When she arrived at her classroom on the first day, her misgivings melted away. She watched Arab and Jewish children interacting simply as children, unaffected by their ancestors' centuries of conflict.

The state-approved curriculum for Israeli schools covered only Israel's history, but Noha integrated Palestinian history into the curricula so that both Arabs and Jews could understand one another's background, and bilingual education so that Jews and Arabs would learn to fluently speak the other's language. She was certain that if Hand in Hand could build cooperation and understanding between Arab and Jewish children, everyone's future would be brighter. "Jews should feel free to enter Arab villages and walk in and speak Hebrew. And I should feel safe to speak Arabic everywhere."

We first met Noha in 2007, when Vital Voices brought Arab and Jewish Israelis together in Derry, Northern Ireland, to learn from the women of Northern Ireland how a country can overcome deep divides to become a united society. Over the decade since the signing of the Good Friday peace agreement, Northern Ireland's women had been integral in pushing the peace out into the community.

Noha heard herself asking the women from Northern Ireland basic questions about the Protestant-Catholic conflict: "What were you fighting about?" She later confessed to me, "I said to myself, *What am I saying? I have heard this question so many times.* It is strange to look at others' conflicts because you learn so much about yourself when you reflect. I looked at the beautiful views and said, *Can't they see above this? Can't they* be *above this?* But we also have a very nice country, a very nice view, and we cannot get above this. I can't get above this. So I take those things with me."

Six years after the opening of Hand in Hand in 1998, Noha became coprincipal of one of four Hand in Hand schools in Israel. In 2009 she took a position with Israel's Ministry of Education as the director of civil and multicultural education. Noha helps both Arab and Jewish schools develop curricula that incorporate the values she instituted at Hand in Hand: community, understanding, and cooperation, which includes the concept of shared citizenship.

Noha sees her students as the future for Israel. "They always say they don't want us to put it on their small shoulders," she admits. "But I have very high expectations that some of them will be leaders in our society; that they will lead us to a different path, to something new, so that we are able to accept both of us in the same land."

Noha's work proves that progress is possible even in one of the most unlikely places in the world. She has bridged the gap between Arabs and Jews by offering the next generation a different view of one another. Perhaps they don't have to be enemies. While these children once lived divided, today they go to school together, speak the same language, and try to view one another not as Arabs or Jews, but as fellow human beings.

LATIFA JBABDI
Morocco

"For more than thirty-five years, I and many of my comrades in Morocco have been planting the seeds of democracy, justice, and peace. Now, finally, those seeds are beginning to bear fruit for the full empowerment of women."

Latifa Jbabdi's organization, Union de l'Action Féminine (UAF), has been working since the 1980s to promote women's rights in Morocco. Her approach to reforming the Moudawana, a family code that relegated Moroccan women to second-class citizenship, had always been secular—until one day when a religious fundamentalist confronted Latifa and her colleagues, calling them infidels. "I remember wondering, *Is Islam truly against the rights of women and girls?*"

Latifa and her colleagues began studying the Koran, reading the text from a woman's perspective. After discovering many Koranic verses that stress equality and human rights, she realized that *sharia*, or Islamic Law, is based upon a set of guiding principles, not judgments set in stone. She and her colleagues reinforced their advocacy arguments on the basis of the essence of Islam and immersed themselves in the Koran, which they discovered could be an influential force for women's empowerment.

In 1992 Dr. Jbabdi's organization launched a campaign to gather a million signatures to reform the Moudawana. They wanted to show people that the Moudawana was not sacred but rather a secular body of law that should be open to debate. Their goal was to raise awareness about gender equality, promote women's rights, and abolish violence against women.

That same year, Islamic fundamentalist leaders issued a *fatwa*, or religious ruling, against Jbabdi and others involved in the campaign. So she developed a counter campaign in mosques in remote cities of Morocco, inciting violence against any who signed the petition. This intense opposition stunned Morocco, which has long been regarded as one of the more moderate countries in the Arab world. Latifa, who had endured imprisonment and torture as a leftist dissident in the 1970s, was not about to back down.

She recalls moments that gave her strength and courage to persevere: "I remember one day, a poor, illiterate woman with no understanding of the Moudawana came to one of our meetings. After talking with us, she became convinced that reforming the Moudawana was her cause too. Soon, she was one of our strongest advocates—knocking on doors and spreading the word."

Throughout her advocacy Latifa relied on Islamic texts from the Koran, together with principles of universal human rights. Eventually, the long years of activism on the part of the women's movement and civil society in Morocco gained the attention of His Majesty King Mohammed VI.

In February 2004 the king adopted landmark reforms to the Moudawana, supporting women, and children, stressing equality, justice, and freedom of choice regarding marriage, divorce, education, custody, and responsibility. The new law guaranteed equal rights and duties for men and women within marriage and addressed them as partners. It represented a structural and institutional change that not only affects Moroccan society but is beginning to ripple across the Muslim world.

Morocco has made democracy and modernity an irreversible strategic choice. With a revised family code, Latifa's country is moving towards a peaceful revolution for women. In 2007 Latifa ran for and won a seat in Parliament. As an elected leader she has worked inside government to implement the law and with the people to spread the word to some of the most remote areas of Morocco. She aims to educate illiterate men and women, who have little access to objective information about the Moudawana reforms and little ability to obtain legal assistance. Latifa wants the people of Morocco to know "the law is a victory not only for women but also for the family, the society, and the generations to come, and that investing in women's empowerment is an investment in Morocco's future."

ODA GASINZIGWA
Rwanda

"In Rwanda today, there are no Hutu women or Tutsi women—only women. What is important is united Rwandan women, creating a stable and prosperous nation for our families."

At the time of the 1995 UN Conference on Women in Beijing, Oda Gasinzigwa's country was just beginning to emerge from the horrors of genocide. In one hundred days, more than one million people had been killed in the Rwandan genocide, leaving women as a large majority of the popuation. It fell to them to rebuild a nation—to restore their agricultural production, reconstruct their homes, bury their dead, and feed their country's children, many of whom had been orphaned.

In the aftermath of the tragedy, Rwandan women, whether Hutu or Tutsi, realized they had much in common. They were trying to support families on the little food and water that was available. They suffered from health problems, trauma, and the burden of HIV/AIDS infections, which had been transmitted to countless women, raped as a strategy of the war.

"When lives were shattered and survival was at stake, when babies were dying and many were homeless, the women of Rwanda didn't think twice about reaching out for another's hand," Oda recalled. In 1995 she and women across Rwanda—Hutu and Tutsi alike—vowed that they would no longer be controlled by violence. Oda understood that if women were going to rebuild their nation they needed to unite and organize themselves. In 2001 women across the country founded the National Women's Council, the largest women's organization in Rwanda. Oda was elected by women at the grassroots level as secretary, and in 2004, elected as president.

Oda and the leaders of the council, with the support of the new government leadership, wanted to do more than restore what had been there before. They wanted a new Rwanda, a Rwanda where every citizen's voice would be heard and respected—including the voices of women. Recognizing that it was imperative that these values be reflected in the new constitution, they drew up a petition outlining women's rights and traveled from village to village to gain support.

"In many countries around the world, I hear familiar stories," Oda explained. "Political leaders promise to protect women's rights and support women's advancement; governments sign on to human rights conventions or new legislation; but without the political will to implement or enforce these laws, real progress is not possible." She and the council were determined to continue to advocate, support, and work with their leaders: the only way to secure a peaceful, prosperous future for Rwanda was to protect women's rights and support their development as leaders in government, business, and civil society.

The Rwandan activists' grassroots initiative to organize women and strengthen their skills, combined with the government's political will to incorporate women's voices into the new constitution, afforded them a place at the decision-making table. In 2003 they pushed to have women leaders represented on the constitutional formulation committee; the women who sat on that committee used their influence to enshrine laws in the constitution to protect women, families, and human rights. Their successes included an equal matrimonial law and the creation of women's inheritance rights. Rwanda's National Gender Policy includes a minimum of 30 percent quota to ensure that women are represented at all levels of government.[12] In fact, as of 2012 women made up 56 percent of the lower house of Parliament, the highest percentage of women's representation in the world;[13] and they also held a number of key cabinet positions.[14]

The parliamentary women's caucus includes women from all backgrounds, who advocate together for women's rights. Economically, they have created microcredit lending programs and communal farms; Rwanda boasts one of Africa's fastest-growing GDPs.[15] They are using the media, particularly radio, to educate the population about issues including HIV/AIDS and violence against women; creating programs to deal with the challenges of HIV/AIDS, malaria, and malnutrition; and mobilizing women and girls to attain an education.[16] In 2008 Oda was nominated by the government as the chief gender monitor in the Gender Monitoring Office.

As of 2011 the women of Rwanda represented the only female majority parliament on the planet, proving by their actions, and by their very existence, that women in government can be the drivers of recovery and the shepherds of a nation. Oda and her countrywomen remain steadfast that the genocide must never be repeated. They are proud to be a model, for Africa and the world, of how women come together across lines that divide to achieve things, even in the most challenging circumstances.

RITA CHAIKIN
Israel

"I encountered so many Russian women in Israel who had been deceived and victimized. At that time no one was defending their rights or taking the problem seriously. Now people are beginning to realize that we were dealing with a phenomenon, not merely a collection of isolated cases, and we needed allies across many sectors to bring change."

Although Rita Chaikin grew up in Israel, she is of Ukrainian descent and speaks both Russian and Ukrainian fluently. In 2001, when she was working at the Rape Crisis Center in the northern Israeli city of Kiryat Shmona, she was asked to counsel women in jail. Stunned to discover how many Russian women were behind bars, she soon realized that these women were not criminals. They were victims of human trafficking, some as young as fifteen years of age.

Soon thereafter, Rita began volunteering with Isha L'Isha (Woman to Woman), which had started a project in the north of Israel to work with women from the former Soviet

Union who, in search of job opportunities abroad, had been trafficked and forced into prostitution. Rita advised them, drawing from her experience in Kiryat Shmona, and in 2002 she was hired to oversee the new project, which included providing trafficking victims with practical, emotional, and legal support, and also a hotline for victims in prison or in brothels.

Rita faced three main challenges. First, it was difficult to build working relationships with the police and to convince them to take the issue seriously. Second, initially, the government was unwilling to get involved. Finally, the Israeli public was poorly informed about trafficking in women. Rita knew that she would need allies from all sectors of society to combat the problem.

To engage the police, Rita made it a regular practice to file official complaints. In each complaint, she offered to train the police in how to deal with victims of violence and human trafficking, thus providing an opportunity for collaboration. She also lobbied police management, knowing that once management was on board, they would communicate down the ranks.

Eventually, the police themselves felt overwhelmed by the burgeoning number of trafficking cases. They turned to Isha L'Isha for guidance and assistance for survivors. Rita worked closely with the police to help them see trafficking for the crime that it is and to treat those who have been trafficked as victims rather than as criminals. She helped ensure that all police attended a lecture on trafficking as part of their basic training.

Out of this collaboration came the Safe Return Program. Prior to a woman's departure from Israel, partner NGOs in the woman's home country as well as the transit city are contacted so that the local NGOs can send a representative to meet the woman and guarantee that she arrives safely home or to a shelter. The NGO can then provide the woman with whatever support, assistance, and rehabilitation are available. Without such support, survivors of human trafficking frequently return to the same conditions that prompted them to be trafficked in the first place.

Just as the traffickers have strong networks, so must those who oppose them. Rita participates in antitrafficking conferences in Russia and Ukraine, as well as other countries of the former Soviet Union, using these opportunities to strengthen relationships, develop new partnerships, and share knowledge.

Rita also works closely with the Parliamentary Committee on Trafficking. A member of the Israeli Knesset once told her, "When we established the committee, most people didn't recognize—even I wasn't fully aware—that we were dealing with a phenomenon, not merely a collection of isolated cases." Rita spent a great deal of time meeting with MPs and other government officials, explaining the realities of trafficking, stressing the need to do more, and offering concrete suggestions for how to do so. As part of the Israeli Coalition Against Trafficking, she has worked with the government to establish a shelter for trafficking survivors who are willing to give testimony in prosecutions against their traffickers.

The U.S. State Department's Trafficking in Persons Report—first developed by Amy O'Neill Richard and now led by Mark Taylor—has helped pressure the Israeli government and many governments around the world to do more to combat trafficking. Only after Israel received a third-tier rating did the government create a law against trafficking in women for prostitution. In fact it was enacted just three days after the list came out. In 2006, thanks to endless NGO efforts, in which Rita took an active role, a new law that targets human trafficking was passed.

There have been strides. The police now see Rita and her colleagues as authorities on trafficking and trust them to identify victims. Thanks to their work, no police officer in Israel is unaware of human trafficking, and police respond immediately when Rita tells them about a woman who needs their help. Rita has also seen positive changes in government prosecutors' treatment of victims. Those who give testimony against their traffickers are offered protection in shelters and are allowed to stay in the country for at least a year. Finally, Rita and her organization have earned the trust of trafficking survivors: today, they pass her hotline number on to others.

In 2010 Rita was invited to testify in Moscow against one of the most prolific traffickers in Europe. She was called as an expert witness to explain the consequences for the defendant's victims. The trafficker was convicted and sentenced to nineteen years in prison; his accomplices received sentences of ten to twelve years. The battle against human slavery carries on. Rita and her colleagues rise and fight the fight anew each and every day.

AFNAN AL ZAYANI
Bahrain

"We were brought here to make the world a better place; each of us must and can contribute."

Afnan Al Zayani is one of the most prominent, energetic businesswomen in Bahrain: CEO of a multimillion dollar company, civil society activist, cookbook author, and host of her own television cooking show. It may not be easy to achieve success as a businesswoman in the Middle East, but Afnan is living proof of the power of determination. When she sets her mind on something, she makes it happen.

And yet for Afnan personal success was not enough; she felt a responsibility to pave the way for other women. In 2002 she took on the leadership of the Bahrain Business Women's Society (BBWS) as a means to connect and give back to emerging entrepreneurs. And in 2006 she and other top businesswomen from across the region decided they wanted to connect with each other to share business strategies and develop new partnerships. "We women entrepreneurs in Bahrain knew that there must be successful businesswomen in Tunisia or Kuwait," she explains, "but we had no means to connect with them." In an innovative public-private partnership between the U.S. State Department, ExxonMobil,

Vital Voices, and businesswomen's associations across ten countries in the region, Afnan helped to establish the Middle East North Africa Businesswomen's Network (MENA BWN), designed to connect, train, and mentor thousands of emerging businesswomen. Top women leaders and executives from the United States and Europe have served as corporate ambassadors, traveling to the region for training symposiums. As a result of the network's support, nearly five hundred new businesses were launched throughout the region between 2007 and 2011. In fact the MENA BWN model led by Afnan and her partners has proven to be so effective that Vital Voices is working with local businesswomen's associations and partners, including ExxonMobil, to replicate it in Africa, Latin America and the Caribbean, and Asia.

Young women throughout the country admire Afnan as a pioneer. Beyond blazing a trail for many budding businesswomen, she has also used her credibility, fame, and vast networks to seek change for unjust laws affecting women in Bahrain. For years NGOs had lobbied unsuccessfully for the government to create a law protecting Bahraini women in cases of divorce, especially regarding child custody. In 2006 Afnan stepped into the debate through her work with the Bahrain Businesswomen's Society. Taking part in a national dialogue, she was able to reframe the conversation in a way that yielded results. With a powerful business platform, her network with the Bahraini Women's Union, and her natural charisma, she contextualized the problem and proposed a national solution, and in language that religious leaders and government officials could relate to. In 2009 the first part of a family law was passed pertaining to members of the Sunni sect. As of 2012 efforts were continuing to bring about the same legal rights for the Jaffari (Shiite) sect so that all Bahraini families can enjoy the same protections under the law. This powerful businesswoman became a heroine of the NGO community, proving that collaboration across sectors can be beneficial to all, yielding faster, more progressive results than either side could achieve on its own.

Afnan's approach has been replicated in many other countries throughout the region: as of 2011 seven advocacy and legal reform projects had been taken up by MENA BWN members. The model has proven that businesswomen can bridge gaps between civil society and government and be effective advocates for change.

Afnan believes "we have to leave a mark" and has made that her driving force. "It doesn't matter whether you are in your home, your village, or running a company. Everyone can leave a mark, and no life will pass unnoticed."

CHAPTER FOUR

BOLD IDEAS AND BOLD ACTION

INTRODUCED BY DIANE VON FURSTENBERG

Designer, and Vital Voices
Board Member

I HAVE NEVER MET A WOMAN WHO is not strong.

I believe there is an inherent strength in every woman. A fearlessness. A leader. Though too often, due to society or circumstance, it takes a tragedy for a woman to realize her power, to truly grasp what she is capable of. Too often it takes adversity to unleash what is always there.

I was raised by a woman with an unbreakable will. Above all else, she was, as every woman at one time or another discovers herself to be, a survivor. My mother endured the injustice and indignity of the Holocaust with grace and resilience. She taught me that "fear is not an option."

The moment a woman decides to be unafraid, she is transformed. When she recognizes the power and possibility of her own strength, and surrenders every fear to that power—she becomes the greatest version of herself. Her character, her passion, her identity—they all come to life.

The leaders I have met in my time as a board member of Vital Voices—Rebecca Lolosoli, Panmela Castro, Sohini Chakraborty, and others you will read about in this chapter—defy the limitations that try to contain them. They are heroines, each of them intent on realizing the potential of their leadership. To read their stories is truly inspiring. Not only did they overcome their miseries, but they used them to help others and to become leaders.

A leader does not hesitate to stake her voice, her freedom, or her safety in allegiance to an ideal. She knows the risk she takes is nothing when compared to the worth she sees in preserving values of equality, compassion, and peace. She sees beyond the risk because she knows that worlds built on injustice cannot stand.

She knows there are no rules or directions; there is no end point. There is only every day. And she chooses to seize it.

n October 7, 2011, news broke that three women leaders had been selected to receive the Nobel Peace Prize in recognition of their "non-violent struggle for the safety of women and for women's rights to full participation in peace building work." Renowned peace activist Leymah Gbowee, whose story of unwavering heroism was profiled in Abigail Disney's film *Pray the Devil Back to Hell*, had mobilized an all-women movement for peace in Liberia. Under Leymah's leadership, Christian and Muslim women united in Liberia, challenging the warlord-turned-president, Charles Taylor, to put a stop to the use of rape as a "toy of war" and end the senseless violence against women. Leymah recalls, "We worked daily confronting warlords, meeting with dictators and refusing to be silenced in the face of AK-47s and RPGs. We walked when we had no transportation; we fasted when water was unaffordable; we held hands in the face of danger; we spoke truth to power when everyone else was being diplomatic; we stood under the rain and the sun with our children to tell the world the stories of the other side of the conflict. Our educational backgrounds, travel experiences, faiths, and social classes did not matter. We had a common agenda: Peace for Liberia Now."[1] Leymah's efforts helped to bring about the 2003 Comprehensive Peace Agreement for Liberia, which paved the way for democracy and stability.

Another inspiring Liberian, Harvard-trained economist Ellen Johnson Sirleaf, overcame years in prison and exile and in 2005 became the first democratically elected woman to lead an African country. In her acceptance remarks, Sirleaf said, "I urge my sisters, and my brothers, not to be afraid.

Be not afraid to denounce injustice, though you may be outnumbered. Be not afraid to seek peace, even if your voice may be small. Be not afraid to demand peace. If I might thus speak to girls and women everywhere, I would issue them this simple invitation: My sisters, my daughters, my friends—find your voices."[2] Under her administration, Liberia has seen a sharp decline in violence and record economic growth.[3] Her voice so powerful, we inaugurated the Vital Voices Global Trailblazer Award in her honor the following year. And in 2011 she was reelected for a second term as president.

The third leader to share the prize was Tawakkul Karman, Yemen's "mother of the revolution." An outspoken journalist, the thirty-two-year-old mother of three had campaigned for freedom of expression and the press in conservative Yemen long before the protests that rocked the country in 2011. "When I heard the news that I had got the Nobel Peace Prize, I was in my tent in the Taghyeer Square in Sana'a. I was one of millions of revolutionary youth. There, we were not even able to secure our safety from the repression and oppression of the regime of Ali Abdullah Saleh. At that moment, I contemplated the distinction between the meanings of peace celebrated by the Nobel Prize, and the tragedy of the aggression waged . . . against the forces of peaceful change. However, our joy of being on the right side of history made it easier for us to bear the devastating irony."[4] Inspired by the Jasmine Revolution in Tunisia, Tawakkul led thousands of youth in protests in Yemen's "Change Square," facing down tear gas, mortars, and gunfire.

These three women share the fourth common trait of world-changing women leaders: When confronted with tough challenges, women put forward audacious new ideas and take bold risks to improve the lives of others. Leaders do not hesitate to voice their opposition in defense of core values or principles, even at great risk to their safety or reputation. Risk is necessary to transformative change, and leaders take it on—not without fear but secure in the knowledge that they are advancing positive change.

At Vital Voices we have found that contrary to gender stereotypes, women are incredibly risk-adept. However, it is worth noting they take risks in very different ways from men. In our experience, women take calculated risks in response to need, as opposed to aggressive risks in response to opportunity. In essence it's not a question of one gender having the guts. It's a question of when members of each gender opt to expose themselves to high-stakes situations. A 2010 study similarly found that "the power to make impact" motivates women to take bold risks.[5]

Sometimes this leadership trait is easiest to see in times of turbulence or crisis. Consider the women-led movement in Argentina during the so-called Dirty War, a period from 1976 to 1983, during which state-sponsored terrorism resulted in the disappearance of thousands of left-wing activists and sympathizers.[6] On April 30, 1977, fourteen old women whose children had gone missing organized a demonstration on the Plaza de Mayo, in front of the Casa Rosada presidential palace.[7] Their protest became a movement, the "Mothers of the Plaza de Mayo," a community of human rights activists who fought to be reunited with lost loved ones.

The Mothers of the Plaza de Mayo wore white headscarves embroidered with their children's names—alluding to their baby blankets—which became a powerful symbol in the shaming of the military dictatorship. As an organization, the Mothers of the Plaza de Mayo bridged social, economic, and urban-suburban divides. The diversity of its membership helped bring together many different communities, breaking the silence that had long characterized the Dirty War.

Or consider the courage and ingenuity displayed by ordinary women in Sicily, Italy, in the 1990s at the peak of Mafia violence and intimidation that permeated the region. The public faced a dilemma: how to resist the Mafia and restore the rule of law while keeping community members safe? The women of Sicily came up with a simple idea: instead of hanging their laundry to dry behind their homes, as was customary, they began to hang white linens on the fronts of their houses to express their anger toward the Mafia and their desire for transparent democratic governance.

Through their networks, women spread the word about the significance of the sheets, and households across the province began to follow suit. Some even wrote the word *Basta*, Italian for "Enough," on the white linens. I was fortunate to visit Palermo during that time and to witness the remarkable displays of grassroots activism. I remember driving through the city, awestruck by the sight of hundreds of white sheets strewn across windows, and shuddering when I came upon the few homes that stood bare. With a simple action, the women of Sicily effectively exposed Mafia members and their sympathizers, a crucial first step toward holding the Mafia and its enablers accountable for their actions.

More recently, we witnessed women taking extraordinary risks to fight for democracy in Ukraine's 2004 Orange

Revolution. The spark was the presidential runoff election that took place on November 21 of that year. Exit polls suggested that the opposition candidate, Viktor Yushchenko, had won handily. But in the hours and days that followed, the incumbent regime brazenly attempted to steal the election, declaring that Prime Minister Viktor Yanukovych had won. By the tens of thousands, the people of Ukraine filled the frozen streets around Kiev's Independence Square to reclaim their democracy. They were ultimately victorious, securing a new election on December 26 and the handover of presidential power to Yushchenko.

Women were at the forefront of that movement, including many who had participated in Vital Voices leadership trainings. One of the most courageous activists was Natalia Dmytruk, the sign language interpreter for the deaf at Ukraine's state-run television channel. Natalia and her children stood with the crowds in Independence Square. Then she would return to work, where she and her colleagues were told to report that the government-backed presidential candidate was the winner.

"I was observing it from both sides, and I had a very negative feeling," Natalia later told *Washington Post* reporter Nora Boustany. "After every broadcast I had to render in sign language, I felt dirty. I wanted to wash my hands."[8]

Disgusted by the deception, Natalia decided she had to tell the truth. At the end of her broadcast on November 24, 2004, she exposed an orange ribbon on her sleeve and, in sign language, told the audience: "Everything you've heard so far on the news was a total lie. I am ashamed to translate these lies. Yushchenko is president. Good-bye. You will probably never see me here again."[9] She was seen again, promptly hired by an independent television station in Kiev.

In each of these diverse situations—Argentina, Italy, and Ukraine—we've seen that the catalyst for change came in large part from women who devised creative solutions and emerged as leaders in times of crisis. In 2011 the world witnessed a similar movement that swept across the Middle East and North Africa. Not only did women stand alongside the men of their countries to campaign for democracy, peace, and greater prosperity, but their courageous actions also helped to spark the fall of authoritarian regimes.

Take for example Egyptian activist Esraa Abdel Fattah. In early 2008, long before the Arab Spring spread across the region, Esraa set up a Facebook group to promote a day of civil disobedience—a general strike and protest of workers' low wages at a textile factory in Mahalla al-Kobra, an industrial city north of Cairo.

Esraa reached out to friends and colleagues, encouraging them to show solidarity with the workers. Online supporters of her "April 6 Movement" grew rapidly from several hundred to more than 77,000. On April 6, 2008, as thousands of workers across Egypt went on strike, the security police cracked down on the demonstrators, killing four. Esraa, known as the "Facebook Girl," was arrested and sent to Qanatir Women's Prison.

The arrest order that landed Esraa behind bars was issued by the Egyptian Interior Ministry. She was the first woman ever to face such an order, and the distinction earned her notoriety as a leader of a growing movement for free speech, civic engagement, anticorruption, and labor rights.

The Facebook group—the networking platform for what is now called the April 6 Youth Movement—changed its profile image to one of Esraa, with the call to action "Free Esraa!"

During her time in prison, and following her release a few weeks later, Esraa became a well-known icon among the political and human rights activists who would later bring down the Mubarak government, aided in part by online organizing tools that empowered ordinary Egyptians to participate in the revolution.

Esraa was part of that revolution, joining other women and men in Tahrir Square to demand an end to an undemocratic regime. But it's crucial to note that taking equal risk in the protests has not carried over to equal representation in victory. In the year following the Arab Spring uprising, women throughout Egypt told us their fears that their voices would remain absent from leadership roles in the judiciary, academia, and key ministerial positions. The military government that was set up after Mubarak was ousted quickly abolished the quota mandating that sixty-four seats in Parliament be reserved for women.[10]

Women across the Middle East and North Africa are finding themselves in similar situations. Like Esraa, women in Tunisia, Yemen, Bahrain, and Libya stood shoulder-to-shoulder with men to demand a voice for every citizen. Women played an integral role in the Libyan revolution, for example, serving on the front lines of change and supporting the rebel soldiers and NATO through such means as nursing, concealing fighters, and smuggling weapons. Now, however, women are finding it increasingly difficult to gain a seat at the table, where they strive to maintain the influence that they gained during the revolution. Having been empowered during the battles against Colonel Muammar Gaddafi, women are increasingly seeking out opportunities for leadership and influence in government, politics, business, and civil society. There is no question women are ready to step up and lead change. Well organized, well led, and well supported, it will be women who ensure that transformation, be it evolutionary or revolutionary, leads to meaningful, enduring change.

The women leaders who have risen up across the region represent phenomenal, emerging shifts—shifts in civic engagement, in politics, in cultural perception, and social interaction—shifts in the very language and means we use to communicate. In Saudi Arabia, online activist Manal al-Sharif openly defied a restriction that denies women the right to drive; she recorded herself driving and posted the video to YouTube, where she became a viral sensation and sparked a national advocacy movement to establish not only women's right to drive, but the dignity and freedom that this right symbolizes. She was jailed for her actions and although released, continues to face intimidation. In Tunisia, Amira Yahyaoui has leveraged her blog following to challenge censorship and mobilize an independent political body to voice the concerns of her nation's youth. In Egypt, Marianne Ibrahim creates a critical space for interfaith dialogue to integrate women and their platform of rights into the transitional government and throughout a fragmented society. In Libya, Salwa Bugaighis resigned in protest from the National Transitional Council; insistent that women's presence was merely nominal and did not equal inclusion or respect, she chose to rally for reform from outside, organizing a contingent of women political candidates for elections. In Yemen, when Shatha Al-Harazi was summoned to meet the president after her tweets caught the attention of the administration, she showed no fear and instead defended her calls for progressive reform, confident that she was representing a rising youth movement. Following the meeting, she was appointed to a university teaching position. Though reform takes time, each of these women, and the countless others that they represent, have broken through in definitive, historic ways.

Just eleven days after the uprising in Egypt, Vital Voices responded to the requests of women from across the region, and assembled women leaders from ten countries from the Middle East and North Africa in Jordan. We wanted to see how we could support them, and they each other. Together we brainstormed about their experiences, their hopes, their fears, and their plans.

Esraa traveled to Amman as a member of the Egyptian delegation. "We need to change how people in our society think about women," she said. "All of society will benefit, not only women. I should participate in building my country." She returned home with support from a network of peers from across the region; the network grew into an advocacy team that crafted and campaigned for a gender platform which could be integrated into the new transitional government.

Esraa has since accepted a position as projects manager for the Egyptian Democratic Academy, a nongovernmental organization that promotes the use of new media tools to foster democracy and human rights values, particularly for marginalized groups. Her goal is to build a women's agenda with input from Egyptian women of all ages, regions, religions, and backgrounds. Meanwhile, the April 6 Youth Movement continues to thrive with more than 100,000 active members. Esraa believes Egyptians must remain true to the principles and values that guided the revolution: justice, freedom, and democracy. "The three main principles we're working to achieve we hope to feel every day," she said. "Not just on paper or in the constitution, but to feel it. We can practice these values every day, in our lives."

• • •

Esraa, women from throughout the Middle East and North Africa, the Nobel Peace laureates, and the women of Argentina, Sicily, and Ukraine are but a few of the many women throughout the world who have boldly stepped up to bring about change. Bold change is one of the most daring, potentially dangerous leadership skills to master. To be successful, women leaders need to also bring the first three leadership skills to their efforts. In each of the previous examples, each leader had a clear sense of mission, a distinct vision for what she wanted to accomplish. In their efforts to effect change, they incorporated cultural signifiers to mobilize the community and applied a participatory approach to their efforts. And in implementing their strategies, they engaged community members as mothers and concerned citizens, effectively bridging social, economic, and geographic divides that might otherwise have overshadowed the protests.

In each case, the women also took significant risks and navigated them in unique ways. The "Glass Cliff" theory was introduced in 2005 by Alex Haslam and Michelle Ryan to describe a trend where women are more frequently tapped for leadership positions when there is a high risk of failure.[11] As mentioned in this book's introduction, Johanna Sigurdardottir, prime minister of Iceland, and the women of Audur Capital were selected to bring Iceland back from financial ruin. But in the aftermath of 2008's global financial crisis, Iceland wasn't the only country to look to women to bring the country back from the brink of economic collapse. When speaking about the global financial crisis, France's former minister of finance and the first female head of the International Finance Corporation, Christine Lagarde, added, "when women are called to action in times of turbulence, it is often on account of their composure, sense of responsibility and great pragmatism in delicate situations." According to a 2010 study, women's ability to connect and empathize is intensified in times of crisis.[12]

This also holds true for the business world. Anne Mulcahy, former chief executive of Xerox, is just one example of a leader who was tapped to turn a company around when it was faced with bankruptcy, a scandal, five consecutive quarters of losses, and $17 billion in debt. She, like the women in Iceland, managed a successful turnaround.

Although this may sound like women are the choice of last resort—given a chance when no one else is willing to step forward for an impossible job—there is more to this trend. In times of great change or crisis, people tend to look beyond the status quo to a new and different solution. During a 2010 political crisis in Kosovo, three different political parties came together to elect Atifete Jahjaga as president. A former police commander committed to building bridges between ethnic groups and rooting out corruption, she had never campaigned politically and never thought she would serve her country in the highest political office.

Working within civil society, in many cases, women are well positioned to take on certain types of risks because they are able to operate under the radar within their communities. By the time their cause is elevated to the public eye, they've already amassed a large group of supporters, as in the case of the women of Sicily, or of Esraa in Egypt. Often the size and diversity of these networks result in a form of protection as women seek to catalyze change.

At Vital Voices we have also found that our engagement with women leaders generates visibility in the media and enhances credibility through high-profile connections with other international leaders. This can be another form of protection. Since 2002 Vital Voices has worked with Anabella de Leon, a congresswoman from Guatemala, whose anticorruption efforts have been a thorn in the side of her government. Anabella grew up poor. She believes that corruption and violence are drivers of poverty and human rights violations in her country. Many of her colleagues have been tortured and even killed. She believes that her affiliation with Vital Voices' global network of leaders, as well as the photo of her with Secretary Clinton which hangs on the wall of her office, serve as a form of protection, letting any would-be attackers know that she is not alone; she is recognized and supported on a global level.

Being bold is about thinking beyond the status quo and having the courage to speak out when others remain silent. Studies have found that a rise in women's participation and in leadership positions in both government and business contributes to greater innovation but also works to decrease corruption.[13] This is because women are not part of networks that traditionally benefit from corruption. Nigerian leader Dr. Ngozi Okonjo-Iweala, for example, is the first woman ever to head the Ministry of Finance, which was the center of the corruption machinery in the Nigerian government. She took the unprecedented step of requiring the ministry to publish the amounts of money it allocates to state and local governments across the country. Because of this change, Nigerians began to realize that public funds actually belong to the public, not to public officers. Armed with the published allocations and aware that the monies are meant to support the Millennium Development Goals, Nigerian citizens are now demanding that their governors and local officials use the resources to provide services to them. Changing decades of corrupt practices is a slow process, but with Dr. Okonjo-Iweala's efforts, the relationship between the governors and the governed is changing for the better. Similarly in Mexico, prominent politician Ruth Zavaleta did the unthinkable: in order to break the cycle of cronyism that excludes women, she sacrificed her seat of power as an act of protest against the endemic corruption she discovered within her own party.

Women leaders' capacity to think and act boldly is evident even in the darkest moments. From Afghanistan to Zimbabwe, I have watched women around the world lift themselves back up after suffering unimaginable violence. I have marveled at their resilience and their resolve to channel their tragic experiences into efforts to save other women and girls from facing the same fate. When I first met Sunitha

Krishnan, the founder of Prajwala in India, she told me she remembered a time when she felt the world conspiring against her. But today, even though she still faces tremendous challenges on a daily basis, she feels that the world comes together in her favor. Among the scores of astounding women Vital Voices has supported over the years, two stand out in my mind for the ways they have defied their fates and reshaped their futures. In 2002, when Mukhtaran Mai of Meerwala, Pakistan, was thirty years old, her younger brother was caught holding hands with a girl from a higher caste. To restore the balance of honor, a village tribunal ordered that Mukhtaran be gang-raped for her brother's offense. The sentence was carried out, and she was left to walk home nearly naked before the eyes of hundreds of villagers. Tradition in such cases dictated that a girl should take her own life in shame. But instead of committing suicide, Mukhtaran reported the rape and fought to bring her attackers to justice. In a landmark verdict that shocked the nation, the rapists were convicted, and Mukhtaran received financial reparations through the criminal justice system.

It was an incredible story, but the most impressive chapter was still to come: Mukhtaran used the money she received to build two primary schools in her village, one for the boys and one for the girls. She believed that education was the best way to overcome the kind of brutality she had endured. Illiterate herself, she enrolled in her own school to learn how to read and write.

Mukhtaran still receives threats against her life, but she refuses to leave her community. As a result of her courage and her fight for social justice, progress has been felt in many villages beyond her own. In 2006 Vital Voices honored

Mukhtaran Mai with the Fern Holland Award, which pays tribute to the memory of a young American woman who went to Iraq in some of its most difficult days to educate Shiite women about their rights and to engage them in the political process. In 2004, at the age of only thirty-three, Fern Holland was shot and killed near Kerbala. Each year we remember Fern's courage and the bold risks she took in fighting for what she believed was right—just like Mukhtaran Mai.

The second woman, Somaly Mam, was an orphan born into the poverty and chaos of rural Cambodia in the 1970s. One day she was approached by a man who called himself her grandfather. She was exhilarated to have found her real family, which had been her dream all her childhood, but the man betrayed her trust and sold her into sexual slavery. Somaly grew up working in a brothel, suffering daily beatings, torture, rape, and humiliation at the hands of her bosses and clients. When a pimp murdered a close friend in front of her, Somaly summoned her courage and fled.

Most women who escape the brothels never look back, but Somaly has made rescuing other girls and young women her life's work. In 1997 she created the nongovernmental organization AFESIP, devoted to the rescue, rehabilitation, and reintegration of girls forced into prostitution. Somaly has organized raids on brothels and brought girls as young as four to her shelters, where they are given the care, education, and training they need to rebuild their lives. Despite continued threats against her life and her loved ones, Somaly has persevered, seeking international pressure to bring the perpetrators of these crimes to justice.

I first met Somaly in 2003 and have traveled to Cambodia many times since to support her work and to connect her with donors and other leaders. On one such trip, Somaly brought us to one of her shelters outside Phnom Penh. There we were greeted with smiles and laughter as Somaly introduced us to the group of eighty girls, all of whom lived at the shelter. But as the girls began to tell their stories, one by one the smiles faded to tears as each relived her own horrors in hearing the experiences of another. One girl told us how she was kept in a hole like a grave, and taken out only to service as many as twenty men a day. Another told us that she was fourteen, pregnant, HIV-positive, and very scared.

Their experiences were brutally painful to hear, much less to have endured. Before our group returned to the United States, I asked Somaly where she finds the strength to carry on. She told me, "It is simple: Love." The love she never had as a child she now offers freely to the girls she rescues.

• • •

These leaders walk among us; in their anonymity, they are made even more extraordinary. Over the years everyone at Vital Voices has been deeply touched, inspired, and humbled by these world-changing women who stay the course even when it means taking extraordinary risks.

In 2005, on the eve of the tenth anniversary of the United Nations Fourth World Conference on Women in Beijing, China, we decided to bring together twenty-five of the most active women leaders in our network. It had been five years since we first brought them together as a global network. Since then—and on the basis of their advice—we had become a nongovernmental, nonprofit organization and had organized scores of training programs on four continents in the areas of human rights, political participation, and economic development. But as we approached the anniversary of that UN conference, we were acutely aware that fundamental roadblocks to women's progress still existed in nearly every country on earth. We could see the change that women leaders we were supporting were making in their communities, but it was an uphill battle because they weren't operating in a world with a level playing field.

We brought the group together to look at how far we'd come and what remained to be done, but also to do some out-of-the-box thinking. We'd been using the same strategies, the same language, and progress globally was slow. Maybe it was time to create, identify, and invest in some new and innovative strategies. To make transformational change for women on a global scale, we'd need to take a page from the women leaders around the world we so admired, who were taking bold risks and achieving impact in their home countries. In effect, as an organization we realized that to break through and create real progress for women, we'd need to dare to risk more ourselves.

Over four days of discussions and deliberations, women leaders from twenty-one different developing countries concurred that whatever the particular problems confronting women or affecting them negatively and disproportionately—poverty and hunger, lack of decent employment and economic opportunity, lack of political power, HIV/AIDS, maternal mortality, violence, climate change—they stem from the same deeply rooted, systemic, and structural causes. They can be attributed to two core roadblocks. First is the lack of *political will.* These leaders identified a great need to strengthen the resolve of governments around the world to enact policies and legislation and commit resources to advance women's rights in their countries. Political will derives from the people in a society and what they demand of government. Not enough people, and especially not enough people of influence, demand that governments act to advance the status of women. So while there may be laws on the books to protect or advance women, those laws go unenforced and under-resourced and are often not taken seriously.

The second challenge or roadblock the leaders identified was far more complex: *women are undervalued within societies*, and this is often deeply rooted in culture and tradition. In many places in the world, women have a different status in society from men and are often considered less valuable. As a result, the institutions of society—legal, social, customary, traditional, attitudinal—ensure that women are inferior and remain so. This inferior status leads to violence against women, the greatest piece of unfinished business of the United Nations Fourth World Conference on Women.

Since 2005, working with the women leaders, we have devised innovative new approaches to some of these age-old challenges. First, to bring about greater political will, we have worked to widen the base of stakeholders who perceive the empowerment of women to be to their own advantage and that of their society. Men, leaders in the private sector and religious leaders, are among those who we knew could galvanize political will. To engage men, particularly in the corporate sector, we'd need to speak their language. So we shifted from a language of fairness or "rights" to make more of an economic case for women's empowerment. We began to strategically and proactively spread this message through every training program and public event, deep into our network. Each year an increasing number of corporations and governments around the world look to advancing women as a matter of economic pragmatism. We are also working to apply the economic argument to violence against women. According to the Centers for Disease Control and Prevention, in just one year in the United States alone, domestic violence costs our economy $8 billion from a loss of productivity and from mental and medical care services.[14]

Deeply rooted traditions of culture are some of the most difficult challenges women face because shifting these ideals is so difficult. Such challenges cannot be addressed from outside the context of a community. We wondered if perhaps those very elements that are responsible for shaping culture—particularly the practice of storytelling—could be a powerful tool in communities around the world. In addition to training, mentoring, and connecting women, we began proactively telling their compelling stories of change through film, photography, and radio. At the same time, Carol Mack, a leading playwright, attended an event organized by a local Vital Voices council of supporters in Connecticut, where Afghan activist Farida Azizi was speaking. Carol became inspired and asked if she could meet other women working with Vital Voices, like Farida, who had incredible life stories of triumph over tragedy. We connected Carol to six other women from around the world, and she engaged six other women playwrights. Over the next few years they developed a piece of documentary theater called "Seven," which has now been published by Dramatists Play Service. The play profiles and intertwines the lives of seven extraordinary women in our network. As of 2012 the play has been translated into twelve languages and performed all over the world. The play focuses unabashedly on traditionally taboo topics, such as violence against women, and has been a powerful tool in communities to open minds and begin dialogue around otherwise difficult issues.

While we have grown into a global organization, we never forget that Vital Voices itself was a bold idea, contrary to the conventional wisdom of its time. In the beginning it was hard to quantify the impact of developing and supporting a leader, but we knew we were on the right path.

Our strategy from the very beginning has been to amplify and support the leaders who are already embedded in a society. We understood that when you develop a leader and unlock that human potential—providing her with new skills, a network of her peers, mentors, and the confidence to achieve her dreams—no one can ever take that away from her. An investment in a leader pays dividends, often accelerating and multiplying over time as that leader touches others. We could see the changes that women leaders were making within their communities, and we knew that their collective capacity to bring change vastly outweighed our own. This notion has inspired us to stay the course, propelled by our own driving force, "invest in women, improve the world," which was coined back at the very beginning by Vital Voices board member Diane von Furstenberg.

REBECCA LOLOSOLI
Kenya

*"You do not have to be educated and you
do not have to be rich to be important
in this world, to make change."*

You can hear Rebecca Lolosoli before you see her. The soft
jangle of her beads and the chime of small coins that hang
from her red cloth *shukka* sound her arrival. Rebecca first
came to Vital Voices in 2008 as a participant in one of
our economic programs, an Entrepreneurs in Handcrafts
Program in Cape Town, South Africa. As the founder of
Umoja Uaso, a village for Samburu women who have suffered
abuse or have been ostracized from their communities,
Rebecca came looking for new ways to market her products.
The women of Umoja support themselves by selling jewelry
they make based on traditional Samburu beadwork.

I personally met Rebecca months later when she traveled
to Washington, D.C., for another of our programs, a political
participation workshop we hosted for African women leaders. Though soft-spoken with a warm, unassuming smile,
Rebecca bears a regal presence. The path she has followed
to leadership has been one she has had to blaze for herself
because women in the Samburu culture are raised to serve
men. In fact when she first learned about the concept of

147

human rights, she stood to the side because she assumed that it simply didn't apply to her as a Samburu woman.

When she was nine years old, Rebecca witnessed the beating of a woman. The woman, who was kind to the children of the village and used to sing and play with Rebecca, did not survive. It was Rebecca's first glimpse of domestic violence. At age nine, she could do nothing. But the memory stayed with her as she set forth to become a defender of peace and community, and a committed advocate for women.

In Samburu culture, a girl is raised to be a wife and mother. Custom condones forced marriage, female genital cutting, and domestic violence. Rebecca saw women endure these traditions, sometimes with shame, always in silence. Often she saw women survive brutal beatings only to be later cast out from their homes and shunned by their families and community. Rebecca saw that these women had no place to go, and many died alone. She reached her breaking point and decided to speak.

When relatives defended violence, calling it tradition, Rebecca protested. She spoke to the elders, to other villagers, to anyone who would listen, and even to many who refused to hear. "Our culture, we like," she explained to me, "but the bad culture we have is always [against] the side of a woman."

Many in her community felt Rebecca spoke too loudly, with too much liberty. Her boldness was an attack on the established hierarchy. Her husband's family felt humiliated, and she was beaten severely and often. Yet these unrelenting assaults only made her more relentless in her fight. She decided that if she could not change the status of women in her own village, she would leave it. She would create a new village, a haven for women who were cast out or needed to escape. On an arid expanse of land in northern Kenya, Rebecca and sixteen women who shared her vision founded a safe space for Samburu women to live with the dignity they deserved. They called their self-sustaining collective Umoja Uaso, which means "United Women."

In 2008 I visited the village along with a delegation of Vital Voices supporters. We were deeply moved by what we found. In a culture where there was no word for protection from domestic violence, Rebecca had created a safe space for women and their children.

Umoja is more than a refuge from violence; it signals an evolution in an ancient culture. In Umoja the language of women's empowerment is spoken with confidence; human rights and economic development intertwine to form a society of peace and progress. The community supports itself through a system of resource sharing. The women make and sell intricate, vibrant jewelry and craftwork, and they pool their income. A sickness and disability fund provides security to those who are most vulnerable, and a school offers an education to the children of Umoja as well as the surrounding villages. Rebecca has even begun to offer training to men on how to protect the rights of women. The village has become a symbol for development and newfound hope; it is her vision, realized.

In 2010 Vital Voices board member and designer Diane von Furstenberg honored Rebecca with our Fern Holland Award for her unwavering commitment to the women of Umoja. That same year the designer featured necklaces from Umoja in her spring collection and stores. Rebecca later told me that the revenue Umoja received from that partnership saved the lives of those in her village, as the Samburu region of Kenya suffered from a debilitating drought that year. As of 2012 the village has grown to more than fifty women and children. Rebecca knows that her daughters will grow into women who cherish tradition but understand it through a lens of equality. Because of Umoja—because of Rebecca—they have the opportunity to live their lives as Samburu; to preserve the best parts of a beautiful tradition and to do so with dignity.

PANMELA CASTRO
Brazil

"People have the power and the right to change culture."

In 1983 a Brazilian woman named Maria da Penha was brutally beaten by her husband and left for dead. The assault left Maria a paraplegic but also turned her into a fierce advocate for women's rights and safety. In the nearly thirty years since the attack, she has become an eloquent voice for thousands of women silenced by the shame of domestic violence. Her experience opened many Brazilians' eyes to widespread physical abuse of women throughout the country—a phenomenon so ingrained in the culture that many ignored it, accepting it as "just the way things are."

One of those people was Panmela Castro. A formally trained artist, Panmela had studied at the School of Fine Arts at the Federal University of Rio de Janeiro and received her master's at the State University of Rio de Janeiro. She then went on to work as a designer. Yet late at night, on the streets of Rio, another form of art called out to her: graffiti.

As a discipline, graffiti is fiercely competitive, territorial, and dominated by men, but Panmela's talent quickly won respect. In contrast to many societies where graffiti is viewed as vandalism, in Brazil it is a respected form of underground public art. Panmela found that graffiti allowed for a highly visible "canvas" for some of her most personal work, provocative images of bold, beautiful women and confident girls. She realized that she could use the visibility of graffiti as a radical public forum for change.

That opportunity came in 2006, when after nearly three decades of domestic advocacy and significant international pressure, the "Maria da Penha" bill was signed by Brazilian president Luiz Inácio Lula da Silva. For the first time, a law codified domestic violence as a violation of the human rights of women and called for public policies to prevent more victims and to punish abusers. As we've seen across the globe, however, a law's passage is no guarantee it will be implemented. Panmela, just twenty-five at the time, wanted to bring attention to the landmark law that Maria da Penha had fought so hard to bring about; a law that radically changed women's rights in Brazil but that few women knew about. She took to the streets, partnering with human rights organizations to turn graffiti art into messages condemning

151

domestic violence in the parts of the city that were home to its poorest women.

Panmela wanted women who suffered abuse to know that they had rights and that there were legal protections for them under the new law. After being introduced to Panmela through Jimmie Briggs—the founder of Man Up, which uses sports and the hip hop culture to engage young men in combating violence against women in their communities—we traveled down to Rio to see her work firsthand. Panmela is cool, perhaps even aloof; yet she is intensely passionate and focused. "I would listen to their word," Panmela told us of her encounters with women who had suffered abuse, "and just knew I could use my art as a way to communicate what I strongly believed: violence is never justified, never right. I thought I could help others see that they have the power to change their situation." Her bright, vibrant murals showed strong women breaking free from oppression. She wanted women to feel empowered to break their silence; and her enormous works on the sides of buildings and highways were impossible to ignore. She explained, "The pictures say, 'My life isn't just on a wall. Learn to respect me, hear my voice. I'm not afraid to speak.'"

Panmela is proof that no matter how young, you have the power to make change. Through Rede Nami, the organization she co-founded that uses art to carry out social projects for transforming culture, Panmela is carrying her message beyond Brazil to women across the world. She continues to work with other artists in Rio, and holds workshops for girls to give them the opportunity to express themselves. Artefeito has developed a following and has become a platform to empower girls to speak out against injustices and understand their power.

"We discuss the law, talk about equality, and about their rights," Panmela says. "We talk about what the murals represent. Always, I tell them that they do not have to be oppressed. The art says what I believe. A woman can be and do what she wants. I represent that idea, and I think that the walls have had an impact—even saved lives."

CARMELITA GOPEZ NUQUI
The Philippines

"When our efforts to work with our own government failed to stop the problem of human trafficking, we turned to Japanese officials instead. We wanted to ask why they could possibly need eighty thousand singers and dancers."

Since the early 1990s, Carmelita Gopez Nuqui has been working with Filipino women who are trafficked to Japan, primarily for forced prostitution. The roots of the trafficking problem date back to the early 1970s, when the government of the Philippines began to certify women as singers or dancers, which qualified them to receive "entertainer visas" from Japan. Each year the number of women sent as entertainers to Japan increased; most of them ended up not as performers but as "hostesses" or prostitutes. Many became pregnant by Japanese men, who frequently abandoned them and their children. For years the Filipino government would not even admit that the problem existed. So Carmelita traveled to Japan six times a year to visit clubs and meet with women who were trafficked. She saw the violation for herself.

In February 1996 she founded DAWN, pioneering a holistic approach to address human trafficking from the Philippines to Japan, and to support victims in rebuilding their lives. First, DAWN committed to supporting women who have already been trafficked. Victims come to DAWN in a state of trauma; they have been abandoned and are often sick. They need counseling, legal assistance, health care, and help returning to their communities. DAWN coordinates their return from Japan and reunites them with their families or provides them with temporary shelter and other psychosocial services. After counseling the women, DAWN provides them with training in alternative livelihoods, such as sewing, hand weaving, and tie-dyeing. Through work, the women regain their lost dignity, and over time transition from victims to survivors. DAWN also provides personal development workshops on subjects such as parenting skills for single mothers. After participating in the program, formerly trafficked women have the tools to become activists and advocates.

DAWN's second approach is to prevent human trafficking through advocacy. For ten years the organization lobbied for an Anti-Trafficking law in the Philippines by attending committee hearings, presenting expert data, and bringing women to share their stories with legislators. When the law passed in May 2003, DAWN worked with the law's interagency committee to represent trafficked women.

The problem was that the Philippines is a poor country, and trafficking provided a major source of income. With this understanding, Carmelita decided to think more creatively: instead of continuing to lobby Filipino officials, she approached the Japanese government, asking Japanese legislators directly how they could possibly need eighty thousand Filipino dancers and singers every year. The Japanese government also faced pressure from the international community to crack down on this form of modern-day slavery, and feared that the upcoming U.S. Trafficking in Persons report would highlight their antitrafficking shortcomings. Legislators were receptive to Carmelita's outreach.

In 2004 I traveled to Japan and met Carmelita; she was part of a program Vital Voices had developed to engage the Japanese government in working with women who combat human trafficking across the region. At that time, DAWN was conducting cutting-edge research and pioneering new, out-of-the-box strategies. She told me how she was starting to take Japanese and Filipino legislators into clubs to see the situation for themselves. Carmelita also invited them to Manila to meet returned women victims and other antitrafficking NGOs. She showed them their data and documents concerning Japan's trafficking violations. Trafficking survivors shared their stories with Japanese officials. Carmelita felt that she was finally breaking through.

As her talks with Japan proceeded, she was able to finally gain the attention of Japanese officials and legislators, and she worked with them to amend their criteria for "entertainer visas." The amendment, which was adopted in March 2005, included provisions that anyone seeking such a visa must prove that he or she has education or experience as an entertainer. Certification from another government is no longer enough. This resulted in a steep drop in the number of entertainers being sent by the Philippines, from about 80,000 in 2004 to about 38,000 in 2005. In 2010 the number of Filipino women deployed to Japan as entertainers was only about one thousand.

Carmelita often hears women say, "Thanks to DAWN, I have recovered a life for myself and my children. I have a way to make a living for my family, and I am now an advocate for other women." Carmelita continues to support women whose self-worth and dignity were shattered in their search for what they hoped would be a better life for their families. She and her organization have expanded their work by reaching out to other Filipino women employed as domestic workers abroad.

LAURA ALONSO
Argentina

*"I think the worst thing you can
do to a corrupt environment
is to behave transparently. You
show people that you can do things
in a transparent way. You tell people
that it is possible to move forward."*

In 1983, when Laura Alonso was only ten, she witnessed democracy return to Argentina after years of state-sponsored violence known as the "Dirty War." During the conflict, an estimated thirty thousand people disappeared.[15] Laura told her father that someday she would study political science and work in politics to help ensure that the democratic ideals so many had fought for would become enduring parts of Argentina's future.

After earning a master's degree from the London School of Economics, she returned to Buenos Aires in 2002 and took a job at Poder Ciudadano (Citizen Power), a leading watchdog organization aimed at highlighting corruption and promoting governmental transparency. Five years later, she was promoted to executive director.

In 2007 I met Laura in Miami at our anticorruption training program for Latin American women leaders. She had become a well-known civic voice, known for uncompromising ethics and for drawing attention to political corruption in Argentina. The U.S. ambassador to Argentina at the time, E. Anthony Wayne, who had been a strong supporter of Vital Voices for years, hand-selected Laura for the program and had told me she was a rising star. More than that, she is a firebrand—persuasive, driven, and passionate—but at the same time sweet and even a little goofy.

In 2008 Laura returned to the United States during the presidential campaign and election; watching the way young people were inspired and invested in the democratic process, she said, "I fell in love with politics again." She returned to Buenos Aires, reinvigorated and ready to make change. After almost a decade spent criticizing the government as an outsider, she decided to enter politics to combat corruption from within. A known progressive advocate, Laura accepted an invitation to run for Congress from the PRO Party, a new, center-right opposition party.

Her candidacy was lambasted by the NGO community and ruling party alike. "As an NGO person you are seen as pure. But when you enter politics, all of a sudden, that changes, and you are viewed as the opposite." Yet Laura was determined to show others and prove to herself that she would stay true to her ideals in Congress. She wanted to prove to civil society and to fellow politicians that leading ethically and democratically works.

She won the election, and in her time in Congress has worked to ensure transparency while not shying away from controversy. Despite representing a conservative party in a society with staunch ties to the Catholic Church, Laura decided not to let her hopes for reelection deter her from taking a stand on polemic issues. "When you are in your [political] party, you are supposed to defend your party. It does not matter if it is something you believe is wrong. I am not that type," she explained. "When I see something wrong, I say it. But I always think of how to make it better. I always present a solution along with what is wrong." In 2010 she was the only one in her party to publicly support the initiative to legalize gay marriage. Her speech delivered on the House floor has since been lauded as one of the key statements that secured the proposal's passage. She has also been a vocal advocate for reproductive rights. And she leads by example. Though Argentina does not require the release of salaries and assets of its public officials, Laura stayed true to her core principles of promoting transparency and combating corruption, personally publishing her salary and statement of assets despite protests from congressional colleagues.

Over time, she has learned to pick her battles carefully. Laura bases her positions on facts and backs them up with evidence. And she does her research. For example, she argued that a male legislator trying to force the resignation of a congresswoman was breaking the law. The quota law in Argentina requires one third of the congressional seats be allocated to women. Laura did not attempt to argue that what the legislator was doing was unfair, spiteful, or undemocratic. While all these things were true, Laura countered corrupt behaviors with a reasoned, fact-based approach. Rather than stand up simply to be heard and be known as a leader, she leads by promoting democratic ideals.

Laura has also found unlikely partners. While she may not agree with many in her party on social issues, they have worked effectively together on issues around transparency. Over time, others in Congress have begun to publish their salaries too. Many people she considered "the enemy" during her time at Poder Ciudadano have since become collaborators and colleagues. "I found that a lot of people here want to do things right," she says. "Sometimes they don't have enough information or the right partners, but they have good intentions."

With her bold opinions and firm convictions, Laura may seem better suited as an activist fighting the system from the outside. But she has proven that she can be a successful politician in an unlikely party, with unlikely partners, and still stay true to her ideals. In large part that is because her goal has never been simply to stay in power. Rather, she is determined to use her power to create change and promote better governance.

GUO JIANMEI
China

"An old Chinese proverb says, 'Women hold up half the sky'—but this is only possible if women can enjoy legal protection and human rights."

Guo Jianmei was also among those exhilarated by Mrs. Clinton's landmark speech at the 1995 World Conference on Women in Beijing. Up until the conference, women's rights violations had not been recognized in China. A legal aid system existed, but women's issues lacked support. At the U.N. gathering, Jianmei learned about the significant role NGOs can play in protecting women's rights. She realized that as a lawyer she had the opportunity and the responsibility to create protections for women in China by providing legal aid.

A few months later, she founded the Center for Women's Law Studies and Legal Services—the first NGO in China devoted specifically to women's law studies and legal services. Combining contemporary international law and traditional Chinese methodology, the center provides services for women suffering from domestic violence and disputes, gender bias in employment, and sexual harassment. When Jianmei began her work, most personal protection laws in China were not enforced. She struggled to gain recognition and enforcement of these laws and pushed for new legislation. She used international laws as models but with the knowledge that any change would have to be grounded in a Chinese context.

In addition to legal reform and oversight, Jianmei realized the center needed to connect with its clients, other NGOs, the media, and government and expand its legal services to include counseling, litigation, research, and advocacy. She created the China NGO Legal Aid Cooperative Group and the China Women's Legal Aid Network, bringing together advocates, lawyers, hospitals, sociologists, public officials, courts, schools, journalists, NGOs, and psychologists in twenty-eight provinces across China. Jianmei's organization also established China's first nongovernmental website and hotline to provide legal services nationwide; in 2005 the center created "Women's Watch-China"—a searchable database and public policy center dedicated to women's rights.

In contrast to standard Chinese legal practice, in which laws are handed down from the national level, Jianmei's approach to legal reform is bottom-up. When she wins a local case, the center promotes the precedent throughout the province with publicity and community trainings. In this way, Jianmei and her staff drive the adoption of new policy from the local level to districts, to cities, and finally to the seat of the province.

I had followed Jianmei's work for a number of years but didn't meet her until 2005, when Vital Voices held a gathering in New York around the tenth anniversary of the United Nations Fourth World Conference on Women in Beijing. At the time, Jianmei reflected on the center's experiences over that decade as "struggling uphill with a heavily loaded cart against a strong wind." Back in 1995 women's rights, legal aid, and NGOs were just emerging in China. The center's staff was working with little experience and modest funds. The traditional, centralized leadership model in China obstructed cross-sector dialogue and made it difficult for NGOs to gain recognition. The staff of the center was facing tremendous pressure as they pioneered new ground.

Yet looking back, the center's lawyers have assisted nearly fifty thousand people and tried more than seven hundred cases, more than half of which have been won. In the past ten years, Jianmei and her team have witnessed a 70 percent increase in women who report human and legal rights violations. Their experience has not always been easy, but Jianmei is confident that China stands at a historic moment in the struggle for women's legal rights.

CHOUCHOU NAMEGABE DUBUISSON
Democratic Republic of Congo

"As a journalist, I found that Congolese women were silenced and I decided to battle for their freedom of expression."

In a June 2011 poll released by Thomson Reuters Foundation's TrustLaw Women, which rated the worst countries in the world in which to be female, the Democratic Republic of Congo (DRC) ranked among the top five.[16]

Civil war has raged across the DRC, the heart of Africa, for many years, with an estimated 5.4 million people killed since 1998.[17] Sexual violence is used as a tactic of war, aimed at destroying communities and removing people from mineral-rich land through intimidation, fear, humiliation, and the intentional spread of HIV. Each year, nearly half a million women and girls are raped. That equates to more than one thousand women each day, causing the United Nations to declare the DRC the rape capital of the world.[18] Women of all ages are gang-raped, raped with guns, and frequently forced into serving as soldiers and sex slaves. Some victims are just a few months old. With no government focus on protecting women's rights and a broken judicial system, there is little or no recourse for women who have been attacked.

Amid this horror a courageous few have mustered the strength to speak out. Chouchou Namegabe Dubuisson is known as a pioneering, fearless voice for justice and accountability. Born in Bukavu in South Kivu Province, Chouchou developed a strong interest in radio broadcasting and journalism as a young student. She saw radio as a way to reach the masses, as it's the only medium of communication in Congo accessible to nearly everyone, everywhere.

Chouchou got her start in 1997 as a presenter at Radio Maendeleo, a popular local community radio station. As Eastern Congo was overcome by violence in the late 1990s,

Chouchou, still in her early twenties, turned her microphone into a potent weapon against the violations of women's human rights, which she saw everywhere around her. In 2003 she co-founded the South Kivu's Women's Media Association (Association des Femmes des Médias du Sud Kivu, or AFEM) to amplify the stories of thousands of voiceless women. She uses radio as a platform to report their attacks, to call for justice, and to help them begin to heal.

Since 2009 Chouchou and her team have interviewed over five hundred women in South Kivu. The stories she heard of heinous crimes carried out against innocent women and children are so horrifying, so unspeakable, Chouchou says she will never forget them. "I met a woman who had five children. They took her into the forest with her children, and kept them there for several days. As each day passed, the rebels killed one of her children and forced her to eat her child's flesh. She begged to be killed, but they refused and said, 'No, we can't give you a good death.'"

With AFEM and through her radio broadcasts, Chouchou shines a spotlight on women's stories, especially in rural areas. She has lifted the plight of Congolese women to the international community by traveling to The Hague in December 2007 to plead the case of Kivu's women at the International Court of Justice.

Chouchou captured my attention in 2008 for denouncing, without fear, the impunity with which major rebel leaders thrive. In March 2009 Vital Voices honored her courage and commitment at our Global Leadership Awards, because we could see that the stories she had to share needed to move beyond the borders of the DRC. In presenting the award, actor, director, and DRC activist Ben Affleck declared, "as long as violence against women—sexual or otherwise—remains strictly and exclusively a women's issue, it will *always* be an issue."

Two months later, Vital Voices joined Senator Barbara Boxer's newly formed subcommittee on women's human rights to host a hearing on Capitol Hill about the violence against women across the DRC. Chouchou returned to Washington to testify:

> Why, why do they fight their war on women's bodies? It is because there is a plan to put fear into the community through the woman, because she is the heart of the community. When she is pushed down, the whole community follows. We also ask, Why the silence of the developed countries? When a gorilla is killed in the mountains, there is an outcry, and people mobilize great resources to protect the animals. Yet more than five hundred thousand women have been raped, and there is silence. After all of this you will make memorials and say "Never Again." But we don't need commemorations; we want you to act now.

It can be difficult for anyone in environments where the worst of humanity persists not to feel overwhelmed or powerless or even become cynical about one's ability to make change. Leaders like Chouchou operate each day in such environments, with hope and determination to turn situations around. And that is the best of humanity. She sees light at the end of the tunnel where others see only darkness. Chouchou once told me, *"When you have nothing else, you have your voice."*

SOHINI CHAKRABORTY
India

"I am not teaching dance; I am inspiring dignity and self-respect."

One sunny afternoon in 1996, dancer and sociologist Sohini Chakraborty wandered through the stalls at the annual Kolkata book fair when a poster caught her attention. It held a picture of a young Indian girl and a poem:

> They sell me my own blood for gold and silver.
>
> I rinse and rinse my mouth but the taste of treachery remains.
>
> I am no more bride to be.
>
> I am no more mother to be.
>
> I am no more future to be.

"I was immediately compelled to go inside," Sohini recalls, "and find out more about the organization. With that action, I embarked on a new journey that would forever change my life."

The poster was produced by an organization called Sanlaap, an NGO in Kolkata that rescues girls who are victims of human trafficking and forced prostitution. When Sohini first arrived at the shelter home, she was stunned to see the girls' faces; their eyes were vacant, and their faces looked much older than their years. Sohini wondered how she could have been blind to the problem of human trafficking when girls were being victimized right in her own neighborhood. After meeting the survivors in the shelter, she wondered what she could possibly do to help.

Six years earlier, when Sohini's mother had died of cancer, Sohini threw herself into dance to help cope with her loss. The next morning, she returned to Sanlaap and offered to volunteer by teaching a dance to the girls. The shelter directors told her it was a crazy idea and it would never work. But Sohini was convinced that dance could be a transformative vehicle for recovery.

At first, many of the girls were so overwhelmed by emotion—from excitement to tears to anger—that sometimes they couldn't even move. "Girls who are the victims of violence and sexual trafficking are extremely uncomfortable with their bodies," Sohini explains. "They don't feel physicality because they feel it is responsible for the stigma attached to them." Traditional means of addressing trauma focus on healing the mind, not the body. Sohini believed that if the girls were encouraged to move their bodies, they could unlock the pain trapped inside and begin a process of healing. "I teach dance movements so that they can learn to love their bodies, to be proud of them and gain confidence to go out into the world and pursue their dreams. The moves help the girls explore what is inside of them, and it helps to get it out."

Soon, Sohini had 120 students between the ages of six and fourteen from the Sanlaap shelter. Sohini was pioneering her own new model, picking up techniques from international practitioners whom she met with on her travels.

"In the brothel, you have no control over your body," she explains. "But when you dance, *you* are the one giving expression to your body. You are controller of your body, of your mind, of your expression. It's freedom."

In 2004 Sohini created Kolkata Sanved, an NGO that teaches dance and works to intercept young people at risk and rural families who might otherwise fall prey to traffickers. As demand for her programs grew throughout India and even in neighboring countries, she launched a program to train survivors to be teachers. As of 2011 Kolkata Sanved has directly assisted more than five thousand women and girls, more than half of whom are survivors of forced prostitution. Sohini organizes public performances and has even created a professional troupe of dancers who travel around the world. She has earned widespread respect within her community, and her efforts give the girls she works with a chance at a new life.

Vital Voices has supported Sohini since 2003, and I feel compelled to visit her every time I travel to India. The first time was in 2004. Sohini met me at the airport, and we set off together in a rickety taxicab. We made a few stops along the way to pick up girls who were part of her program—survivors who had been trained by Sohini and now were teachers themselves.

As we left the noisy, polluted city, we turned off the crowded highway and down a dirt road, finally arriving at a collection of small buildings surrounded by palm trees. While I received a tour of the property, Sohini gathered a number of the girls for their rehearsal. But it was clear there was something else going on. Sohini pulled me aside and told me that one of the girls in the shelter had died the night before. She had been just twelve years old, and like many shelter residents, she had been HIV-positive. Other girls were asking Sohini when it would be their turn to die.

That day helped me understand what Sohini is up against. She is facing an epidemic that seems to have no end in sight, and she is dealing with new trauma that emerges on a daily basis. Her methodology helps to heal through the expression of pain, but that also means some of the darkest memories must be surfaced and relived.

She has come a long way. People no longer tell her she is crazy. Sohini continues to be driven by two dreams: she wants the world to see these girls as survivors, not victims; and she hopes to one day start a global institute where creative therapy can be taught and shared with people from around the world. I know she will.

CHAPTER FIVE

PAYING IT FORWARD

INTRODUCED BY MELANNE VERVEER

Ambassador-at-Large for Global Women's Issues, U.S. Department of State, and Vital Voices Co-Founder and Chair Emeritus

IN RECENT YEARS, WE HAVE SEEN A meaningful shift both in perception and practice of the role of women advancing economic, social, and political change. Today women are at the center of diplomacy and development efforts, no longer just as beneficiaries but as agents of change.

All around the world, women are blazing new trails and triumphing over long-entrenched obstacles in the pursuit of creating a better world. Empowered women are one of the most effective and positive forces for reshaping the globe. We know that when women progress, everyone benefits: men and women, boys and girls.

As women become empowered, they empower their communities. They exercise the kind of power that is not power *over*, but power *for*. They share new knowledge, skills, and resources, and invest in the education and leadership training of the rising generation. Women "pay forward" their successes to their community. They give of themselves; they understand that progress is a shared endeavor. It is one in which we all have a stake. The leaders I have met through Vital Voices—some of whom are profiled in this chapter—are women like Danielle Saint-Lot of Haiti, Jaya Arunachalam of India, Maria Pacheco of Guatemala, Andeisha Farid of Afghanistan, Liron Peleg-Hadomi and Noha Khatieb of Israel, Kakenya Ntaiya of Kenya, and Samar Minallah Khan of Pakistan. They have a remarkable capacity to lift up the most vulnerable among them, to raise the voices of those who have been silenced by circumstance, and to make a difference.

It is their extraordinary commitment to a cause and to a vision that extends beyond the individual which makes these women exceptional leaders. Each leads for others. Their work will survive each of them because it is never about one woman's solitary journey. There are no solitary journeys. Their leadership has been rooted in securing a better future for the next generation.

Gender equality has rightly been called the "moral imperative of the twenty-first century." The struggle is far from over. Women leaders like these—the vital voices of our time—are hastening progress on the road to equality for women and girls, and in so doing, creating a better world for people everywhere.

I n 2008 I traveled to Guatemala with a Vital Voices delegation to visit Maria Pacheco, whom I introduced in Chapter Two. She had said to me over the phone, "You will never understand the impact that Vital Voices has had on me until you see what I have been able to do for the people of my country." In 2006 Maria had returned from the Vital Voices training program in Washington, D.C., anxious to spread the knowledge she had gained with women across Guatemala. But more than knowledge, she wanted to spread her vision of a better future, a vision that for the first time had been acknowledged and supported, she felt, by our investment in her.

She reached out to other women leaders in Guatemala with the idea of launching a Vital Voices chapter aimed at mentoring and training hundreds of young women across the country. As she built support, she spread the idea to women leaders throughout Central America, telling them about Vital Voices and encouraging them to replicate her model in their countries. Over the next two years, we were invited to Vital Voices chapter launches in Honduras, Nicaragua, El Salvador, and Panama. Our initial investment in Maria was paying benefits for women and societies across the hemisphere.

Joining Maria in Guatemala for the launch of the regional network reinforced something I have seen around the world: women leaders have a powerful need to "pay it forward." Maria, like so many other women leaders I have encountered through Vital Voices, seeks power for the purpose of empowering others—for lifting others up rather than keeping others down. Simply put, they have a vision that extends beyond their personal achievement. I've seen it firsthand in chain reactions that women leaders have set in motion around the world.

The women that Vital Voices supports pursue leadership not to amplify their own power, influence, or wealth but rather as a vehicle for promoting positive change. This leadership approach is characterized by the four principles described thus far. A defined sense of mission drives leadership activities intended to have positive impact beyond the leader herself. Listening to and learning from the community enables a leader to act inclusively, addressing the perspectives of all who share a stake in the outcome. Seeing the potential for constructive impact encourages bold ideas and bold action. And putting it all together creates a new paradigm of leadership, one that understands power not as something to be hoarded but rather as something that expands when it is shared.

Traditionally regarded as nurturers, women have been conditioned—and some might argue, have a biological inclination—toward holistic thinking.[1] This aspect of women's socialization puts them in a unique position to create lasting change. As nurturers of the next generation, women understand that change can only be sustained when rising leaders are also groomed to sustain it.

Madeleine Albright has often been heard to say, "there is a special place in hell for women who don't support other women." At Vital Voices we've been struck by the opposite trend: the active willingness of the women leaders we support to share their knowledge, skills, and resources through volunteerism and mentoring. It is almost as if they can't wait for the opportunity to give back. A great example of this came in 2007, when founder and former CEO of Oxygen Media, Geraldine Laybourne, met with a group of our mentees from around the world. She told them a story about how young women were constantly calling her assistant trying to take Gerry to lunch or coffee to seek her advice on their careers. As Gerry was overwhelmed with the requests and the demands of a growing company, her assistant would tell the young women that Gerry didn't "need another meal or to interrupt her day—she needed exercise." Gerry started a practice of meeting young women each morning in Central Park and offering advice as they walked. One day she recalls telling her vice president Andi Bernstein, "Hey, here's an easy-to-do idea . . . let's gather women, just a few hundred, in Central Park and get our high-placed women friends [who happened to be Meryl Streep, Diane von Furstenberg, Heidi Miller, among others] to mentor younger women. Maybe we can get media coverage and show how women do help women." As Gerry went on to describe the dozen or so Mentoring Walks that were organized around the country in the next few years, I looked around the room and could see Gerry's story taking hold in everyone who was listening.

Sure enough, a few months later those same young women, back home in their own countries, began organizing mentoring walks of their own, gathering the top women leaders they admired to walk with and mentor promising young women. With inspiration from Gerry, the concept "if you light another woman's candle it does nothing to diminish your candle . . . you get more light and more heat" has truly gone global. And it has stuck. On the third Saturday in November each year, women—established and emerging—walk together in their communities. Each walk is followed by programs to initiate mentoring partnerships and foster the leadership potential of aspiring young women. To date, Mentoring Walks have reached thousands of women across four continents. In 2009 Gerry traveled with us to participate in the Mentoring Walk in Kampala, Uganda, organized by alum Rehmah Kasule, and in 2010 she joined us in Buenos Aires for the walk led by Maria Hoch and the Vital Voices chapter in Argentina.

Women leaders relish the opportunity to connect with something global, which has tangible benefits to their local communities. In 2010 Vital Voices leader and entrepreneur Zoe Dean Smith was troubled by the staggering statistics in her country: 49 percent of young women aged twenty-five to twenty-nine in Swaziland are HIV-positive.[2] And the problem is getting worse. The majority of new infections—62 percent—occur in females.[3] Multiple interventions by the government and international community have failed to make an impact, and she could see that the problem was suffocating her country's economy. Zoe knew she needed an out-of-the-box solution. In 2010 I traveled to Swaziland to join Zoe for the launch of her mentoring program, which brings high school girls together with successful women entrepreneurs. Through the mentorship experience, she is aiming to model a different road map for the girls. It is too early to know the full impact of this intervention, but Zoe can already see progress. The mentorship experience has had undeniable impact.

Through Vital Voices, I have engaged countless women leaders in discussions related to the origins of their success. In almost every conversation, the leader attributes her achievements to an individual or group of individuals who empowered her to realize her potential. These supporters may have been female or male; colleagues, family, romantic partners, or friends. The characteristic they have in common is that they acted as mentors—and for that, they receive immense and enduring gratitude from the women they supported.

There are clear reasons for this. Simply put, there aren't enough role models for talented and aspiring women in public and private life around the world. Because of this, women often feel isolated and doubt themselves until their dreams and abilities are recognized or validated by external forces. Susannah Shakow, the president of Running Start, often reminds me that even in the United States "women, on average, need to be asked seven times before they seriously consider stepping up to run for office, while men generally have enough confidence to jump into a campaign with little outside encouragement." She founded her organization to be the "first ask" to politically promising high school girls. At Vital Voices we have found that when women are encouraged to step up and lead change, they mirror this behavior of believing in others and helping to building their capacity.

As Vital Voices came to recognize women's desire to share the benefits and investments we were making in them, we started deliberately building the concept into our ongoing work. We told each new group of Vital Voices women the stories of other women we had worked with in the past, and how those women had used their new skills and contacts to "pay it forward." As we had hoped, the idea resonated.

In 2008, for example, a confident Ghanaian business-woman, Brigitte Dzogbenuku, participated in the Fortune / State Department Global Mentoring Program. Her goal was to enhance her skills and contacts so she could bolster her career as a sports club manager. After a month-long mentor-ship with Donna Orender, who was at that time the president of the Women's National Basketball Association, and after hearing Maria Pacheco's story, her goals expanded. On the last day of the program, Brigitte announced to the group, "I came here thinking only what I could gain to be a greater success in my career. I am leaving here knowing that I am a leader, thinking only about my community and how I have the opportunity and responsibility to invest in the next generation of girls in my country."

A few months later, we visited Brigitte in Accra, Ghana. In the interim she had founded Hoop Sistas, a basketball mentoring program for young women. Brigitte knows that lessons learned on the basketball court—self-confidence, discipline, collaboration, and healthy ambition—are also lessons that girls can apply to win in the game of life. The Hoop Sistas program combines sport with educational workshops on career development and women's health, and Brigitte uses the program to bring girls together to tackle bigger issues: the local and global challenges that threaten women's progress. "I want these women to be empowered; to be able to stand their ground, to hold their own, to help other people," she stated. "Women in Africa need to realize how powerful they are."

Increased attention has been paid to the types of investments in women and girls that foster the greatest returns. In our experience at Vital Voices, investments in human capital through training, education, and capacity building yield profound returns, especially when coupled with efforts to build a woman's social capital by providing her with mentors and a global network of peers and supporters.

For example, in the case of Brigitte Dzogbenuku and Donna Orender, it wasn't just that Donna's example helped demystify the process of succeeding in a sports career. By sharing her own contacts with Brigitte, Donna gave her access to social capital she would have had a hard time building on her own. At Vital Voices we call this "borrowed social capital," a term often written about by Professor Ron Burt at the University of Chicago.[4] These relationships greatly increase a mentee's confidence and sense of support. Research has also shown that mentors can help foster an environment conducive to creative experimentation. And it's a virtuous cycle: risk-taking, particularly when it is backed by strategy and support, further develops an emerging leader's self-confidence.

In 2010 *Harvard Business Review* released a study questioning the value of mentoring and pointing to the fact that men in the corporate world were strategically "sponsored" rather than "mentored," enabling them to more quickly climb the corporate ladder.[5] Sponsors go beyond giving advice; they advocate for their mentees. Sponsorship in corporate America is important. But the need for mentoring is real. Aspiring women leaders and entrepreneurs in Africa, Latin America, Asia, and across the Middle East often report that they feel isolated. They struggle to connect, share best practices, and develop partnerships outside their local environments. With only a few women in top leadership positions in their home countries, it has been even more challenging for them to identify successful female role models to emulate—a challenge compounded by the social, economic, legal, and cultural barriers women still confront in many countries.

This challenge opens up opportunities for global mentoring to make a real impact. For the first time in history, there is a generation of established women leaders looking for ways to give back. They want to do more than just invest financial resources; they want to give their time, talent, and passion, and most of all, their experience. Vital Voices mentor and global vice chair of Ernst & Young Beth Brooke has said, "to make a difference as a mentor or a sponsor you've got to commit to active participation in a young person's future with skin in the game." Many women at the top have developed powerful networks, which can be leveraged around the world.

For example, in 2011 Vital Voices board chair Susan Davis, a successful entrepreneur, and Anne Finucane, chief strategy and marketing officer at Bank of America, began a discussion about the value of investing in women. Both were involved in Irish causes, and since the early 1990s both had been working with the people of Northern Ireland to support the peace process. Although progress had been slow, following the Vital Voices conference in Belfast in 1998,

Anne witnessed the power of women leaders to transform their societies. She was now looking to develop an initiative within Bank of America that would have global reach and tangible results. Our two organizations have collaborated to launch the Global Ambassadors Program (GAP), designed to close the global leadership gap by tapping top women leaders in business, government, media, and civil society to serve as mentors for the emerging women leaders Vital Voices supports worldwide. The program was launched by the bank's CEO Brian Moynihan in March 2012 while working with a group of women leaders in Haiti to develop their nation's first-ever National Platform for Women—sending a clear message, from the top, of the company's commitment to women's leadership to advance countries and communities.

Vital Voices' mentorship programs are designed to transform the leadership paths of the women we serve. We have found that mentorship enables emerging leaders not only to see high-level leadership in action but also to understand that leadership is simultaneously an opportunity and a responsibility. We have found that emerging women leaders who are mentored feel a greater responsibility to take what they've gained and "pay the experience forward" than those who were only provided training—a trend confirmed by an organizational behavioral study which found that mentees are far more likely than nonmentees to become future mentors themselves.[6]

At Vital Voices we see an interesting trend among some of the most exceptional women leaders we support, namely that they want our help in creating a leadership pipeline to develop their one-day successors. This practice of "replicating oneself" is seen among leaders who understand the importance of sharing power and platforms with others to benefit the larger cause. Back in 2010 women in our network, such as Sunitha Krishnan and Somaly Mam, approached Vital Voices vice president for human rights Cindy Dyer and asked her if Vital Voices could help them develop the leadership skills of the women who will succeed them. As a former prosecutor who has dedicated her life to bringing perpetrators of violent crimes against women to justice, Cindy understood the personal toll and the grave risks these leaders face. So she set out to create a program to address this need.

This model of "replicating oneself" has been seen not only among human rights leaders. Vital Voices mentor and top Fortune 500 executive Anne Mulcahy captured headlines when she made public and built a highly effective partnership with her successor Ursula Burns years before her own departure as chief executive of Xerox. Cause-driven leaders understand that their vision for change is bigger than themselves and that they will need to cultivate others to carry the mission forward.

One of the trends that inspires us most at Vital Voices is when women leaders whom we have trained and supported not only reach out and mentor others in their own communities and organizations but step up to support other women in our network. Since our founding days we have watched women organically take practical models for creating social, legal, or economic change from one region and replicate them in another. But women in the network have also supported one another on an individual level in times of great professional or personal crisis. In August 2009 Rebecca Lolosoli and the Umoja Uaso Women's Village suffered a violent attack. Rebecca's estranged husband showed up in Umoja armed with a gun, and assaulted Rebecca. He stole valuables and claimed that village land held in Rebecca's name rightfully belonged to him. He threatened to kill her over money earned from increased sales of Umoja's beadwork.

Samburu villages are protected by fences made of thin sticks. It's a perimeter designed to keep out wandering wildlife, not agitated gunmen. Rebecca contacted the local police, but claiming this was a domestic dispute, the police did not respond. Without any meaningful security options, Rebecca—the chief of the village—left, reaching out to the network of Vital Voices women leaders throughout Africa. The group responded immediately and with determined coordination, first providing Rebecca with a safe place to stay, medical care, and legal support. They used their network to get media attention around the issue and to advocate for legal change with local and national networks, and they took Rebecca's case to political and human rights leaders. A clear message was sent to Rebecca's husband, and to the police who tried to ignore her report, that she has a powerful network of support throughout the country, the region, and around the world. The path of leadership is sometimes a very thorny road. Marina Pisklakova of Russia has often said, "Vital Voices is taking care of those who are taking care of the world." Emerging leaders need mentors to guide them, but they also need a network of peers to reassure them that they are not on the path alone.

DANIELLE SAINT-LOT
Haiti

"We don't just want to rebuild;
we want to reimagine a new
Haiti . . . where women's contributions
are valued, our voices are
heard, and our rights are protected."

The third Vital Voices conference, which took place in Montevideo, Uruguay, back in 1998 when Vital Voices was still a U.S. government initiative, brought together more than three hundred women from across the Western Hemisphere to discuss challenges including human trafficking and the growing number of gang-related femicides; as well as the lack of women's representation in the political sphere and labor force.

Danielle Saint-Lot attended the gathering with six other Haitian women. They found it inspiring to hear women policy makers from across the Americas describe successful strategies in reforming penal codes and passing antidiscrimination legislation, and judges and prosecutors share best practices for laws that classify domestic violence as a crime.

"We wanted to bring the seeds of Vital Voices back home," Danielle recalled, "but more than that, we wanted to be part of something that was bigger than ourselves—a global movement for women's progress."

Danielle also felt that Haitian women faced unique challenges. I first met her at that conference, where she told me that she and the other Haitian attendees were planning their own Vital Voices gathering in the following year. Backed by the U.S. embassy in Port-au-Prince, Danielle and her colleagues launched the Hundred Haitian Women for Vital Voices, which resulted that same year in the creation of the very first Vital Voices chapter, Femmes en Démocratie (FED).[7] FED's goal was not only to bring the ideas of Vital Voices to the women of Haiti but also to translate the mission into tangible local solutions that would serve the urgent needs of Haitian women.

Even before the devastating earthquake of 2010, Haiti was the poorest country in the Western Hemisphere, with more than 80 percent of the population living below the poverty line and 54 percent in abject poverty.[8] Two-thirds of all Haitians depend on the agricultural sector for their livelihoods, mainly small-scale subsistence farming.[9] Their well-being is threatened by frequent natural disasters, which are further exacerbated by widespread deforestation. Haiti suffers from a severe trade deficit and a lack of investment because of security concerns and limited infrastructure; remittances total nearly a quarter of GDP and more than twice the earnings from exports. The government relies on formal international economic assistance for fiscal sustainability. Amidst these desperate conditions, Danielle recognized that many women across the country were not even aware of their human rights. Consequently, one of the FED's first projects was a handbook, *Haitian Women's Human Rights from A to Z.*

Danielle and her colleagues were also concerned that women's voices were not represented in government. In fact Haiti ranks among the lowest in the world for political participation, with women holding only 3 percent of seats in Parliament. Women who sought political office were frequently subject to intimidation, even death threats. Danielle told me, "Haiti is a country with a fractured political system. We are a country with more than thirty political parties. People aren't used to seeing anyone come together across these divides. We wanted to be an example for what could be in Haiti." Taking a page from the Northern Ireland Women's Coalition, FED brought women candidates together and supported their campaigns. In a 2006 election, FED supported, with training, fifty women running for political office from different political parties. When the women journalists reporting on corruption or human rights violations received threats, FED members opened their homes to offer protection.

The chapter also lobbied parliamentarians for greater participation of women in government. In 2011 a constitutional amendment enshrining a 30 percent quota for women at all levels of government was passed. Between 1999 and 2011 FED trained over three thousand female microentrepreneurs and developed a network of over five hundred women electoral observers. "Women's voices were rarely heard, but our connection to Vital Voices opened doors and people began to listen," said Danielle. FED's efforts to empower women across the country earned support from the U.S. embassy, the Inter-American Development Bank, European Union, UNDP, and even the private sector.

In November 2009 I traveled to Port-au-Prince to celebrate the chapter's tenth anniversary. While there, I was able to participate in their seventh annual trade fair, which showcased the work of women artisans and entrepreneurs and connected them to buyers and export markets. Six weeks later, on January 12, 2010, the mood of celebration was abruptly shattered when a 7.0 magnitude earthquake brought the country to its knees.

Despite their own losses, Danielle Saint-Lot and the women of Femmes en Démocratie leapt into action. Within twenty-four hours Danielle was in communication with Vital Voices, discussing how women, so often the victims in times of crisis, needed to be at the center of reconstruction. "In Haiti, there is increased focus on building the infrastructure and investing in business," she told me. "This is important, but we must also invest in the people. Women must be central to this process." Danielle organized a camp near her home in Jacmel, in one of the most devastated areas, where she and her daughter provided shelter, food, clean water, and medical support to others in need.

The international community rallied behind Haiti, but recovery has been agonizingly slow. Two years after the 2010 earthquake, people were still living in crowded, unsecure, and poorly lit camps, often lacking basic sanitation and access to water and food. Women have been subject to sexual violence, as political instability and weakened institutions create a climate of impunity for rapists.

Yet despite scarce resources, women have established security patrols and provided community support, legal advice, and medical care for rape survivors. Most important, when disaster struck, the network of leaders Danielle had created was strong. Together they were able to respond quickly and broadly to the spectrum of issues confronting Haitian survivors. Femmes en Démocratie provides a channel to support the needs of women locally and is simultaneously bringing Haitian women's voices to the international community, connecting them with partners around the world.

NOHA KHATIEB AND LIRON PELEG-HADOMI
Israel

"I think their relationship proves the way it could be. The way the partnership could be between women, between people."

Liron Peleg-Hadomi is a community social worker in Israel. From the time she was a university student, Liron has worked with NGOs committed to strengthening relations between Jews and Arabs in Israel and coordinates cross-sector and cross-community leadership programs such as LEAD Haifa.

Noha Khatieb, featured in Chapter Three, has helped bridge the gap between Israeli Arabs and Jews, serving first as a teacher and then principal at an integrated school, and since

2009 as the director of civic and multicultural education for Israel's Ministry of Education.

The two women met in 2007 in Northern Ireland as participants of Vital Voices' "Peace and Prosperity" program. Though Liron is Jewish and Noha is Israeli Palestinian, the two immediately connected in the cab ride from the airport to the program site. Despite holding divergent views on contentious issues, they quickly became friends. Liron had come to Northern Ireland newly pregnant. Noha looked after her and fussed over her comfort. Not long afterward, Noha learned that she too was pregnant, with twins. The two women remained close throughout their pregnancies after they returned home to Israel and even gave birth just one day apart. What started as a friendship, bonding as mothers, has developed into a powerful partnership in support of a shared society.

In 2010 Noha and Liron brought the Vital Voices Peace and Prosperity program back home to Israel, where they are now helping others cross the lines that divide. Working with twenty young Israeli women—ten Jewish and ten Arab—the program they've designed facilitates connections and collaborative community projects. Under the coordination of Liron and Noha, the participants attended eleven gatherings over the course of a year on topics such as developing cross-community dialogue skills, exploring narratives in action, turning ideas into projects, project management, and using media to achieve social change. The meetings stimulated candid dialogue and sharing of perspectives. Most important, it allowed a new wave of leaders to engage with those they never expected to connect with. Many participants credit the program with allowing them to put preconceived notions and prejudices aside and see one another simply as women. Women who never would have interacted with one another have been able to forge professional connections and personal friendships, just as Noha and Liron did.

"This is how change starts," Noha says. "I believe in the small steps. These drops will eventually bring the big rain. And it will come. I believe." Tensions in Israel will not be erased overnight, but the more people there are working towards peace, the sooner it will come. Noha and Liron set the ultimate example for the women they help to lead. "It's as if they complete each other," offered one participant. "Not only the fact that one is Arab and one is Jewish. They also set a very good example of coexistence." Liron sums up the strategy in three simple words: *connections, relationships, impact.*

ANDEISHA FARID
Afghanistan

"I feel that I have a duty to do something for the Afghan people, for the children, and for our future."

Born in Afghanistan during the Soviet occupation, Andeisha Farid spent her childhood in a refugee camp in Iran, where her parents fled with Andeisha and her seven siblings. She remembers arriving at the camp as a young girl to discover no drinking water, no medical facilities, no food, and nowhere for children to play. Unable to attend school, Andeisha was surrounded by poverty, illness, and death.

Her parents managed to send her to Pakistan to another refugee camp, where she was at least able to go to school. While studying there, she decided to tutor other Afghani women and children who weren't as fortunate. In 2002 Andeisha moved to Islamabad to attend university. There she worked again with a local Afghan community, first as a teacher and later as administrator and spokesperson of an Afghan school. But Andeisha dreamed that one day she would return to Afghanistan to help the people of her native country. A child of Afghanistan, a product of refugee camps, Andeisha had achieved a quality education. She wanted to show that other Afghan children could have a future too.

In 2004, when she was twenty years old, Andeisha started her first orphanage in Kabul. Most of the children weren't technically orphans. They had parents who would have liked for them to get an education, but out of economic desperation they were sent to the streets to beg. "These children motivated me," Andeisha says. "They wanted to be in school; the families wanted them to be in school."

By 2011 one orphanage had become eleven: five of them in Kabul, four in other parts of Afghanistan, and two for Afghan refugees in Pakistan. Through them Andeisha supports hundreds of Afghan children. Most arrive at one of her orphanages between the ages of six and nine, having already lived through desperate poverty or severe trauma, from witnessing horrifying events to suffering abuse. "I don't see in them these things," Andeisha insists. "I see a future teacher, doctor, journalist, lawyer, officer. I see the possibilities in them." At her centers, the children play sports, get schooling, do chores, and eat their meals together as a communal family. Some even apply for scholarships to study abroad. One girl arrived at the orphanage scarred, afraid, and mute. She would not communicate with anyone. After eight years in Andeisha's care, she earned a scholarship to study for four years in Italy. Today, she speaks five languages.

In 2008 Andeisha was selected as one of the first of Goldman Sachs's 10,000 Women Fellows and was provided a business and management education from the American University in Kabul. She runs her orphanages with a CEO's precision and savvy, and she considers the children her clients.

"Doing this warms my heart. Somehow at the end of the day, when I close my eyes, I know I have done something. It keeps me moving; it gives me hope." Andeisha's driving force is a firm belief that *education is a stance against oppression.* She has seen children transform their lives against the odds. She strives to replace their memories of suffering with a sense of belonging and equality. She hopes that they will come to love their country as much as she does; that they will grow up with the skills and values to return Afghanistan to its former glory and national dignity. She wants them to be proud of their homeland and confident in themselves. "If we can raise our children to give them that future, I will do it."

KAKENYA NTAIYA
Kenya

"I see girls with big dreams. Yes, these girls will be vital voices in our society. It is my dream to bring them this future of hope."

Kakenya Ntaiya was engaged to be married at five years old. Her parents had chosen an older boy from the village and had concluded a contract with his family, promising her to him when she was twelve or thirteen, old enough to become a bride. In the Masai ways of Enoosaen, Kenya, this is the way things are done. "When a girl is old enough to walk, she's taught how to sweep the house, how to collect water from the river; she's taught how to milk the cows, to fetch firewood, and to cook for the family. A girl is raised to become a wife and mother. A boy is raised to become a warrior," Kakenya explains. "These are traditions that my people have followed since before anyone can remember."

Kakenya is the oldest of eight siblings, which meant she had to help her mother raise them. Her father worked as a policeman in the city and was away for weeks or months at a time. When he did come home, he frequently beat her mother, sold the family's livestock, and used the money to get drunk. "My mother's life was very hard," Kakenya says. "I knew that I wanted something different."

193

If her chores were done, Kakenya was allowed to go to school. Masai girls in Enoosaen commonly attend primary school, though their education is taken less seriously than that of boys because no one expects them to go much beyond the seventh or eighth grade. "When a girl becomes twelve or thirteen years old, there is a ceremony. We are told that this ceremony will make you a woman, and once you are a woman you can get married. I was considered lucky because I already had a husband waiting." The ceremony is the Masai practice of female circumcision, often referred to as female genital cutting. In Masai tradition, the ritual marks the transition of a girl into womanhood and signals her readiness to become a wife. In practice, marriage means the end of a girl's education, because she is expected to take on the roles and responsibilities of caring for the household and her husband, and to begin having children.

Kakenya confesses she didn't feel lucky to have a husband-in-waiting. She loved school. The teachers who came in from other communities to teach the Masai children seemed glamorous and important to her. She remembers, "I dreamed of being a teacher because the teachers wore shoes and had different clothes each day. Teachers didn't have to work on the farm."

So as the time approached for Kakenya to undergo the cutting ceremony, she played the only card she could think of. By custom a girl was not permitted to address her father directly. She should have asked her mother to speak to him on her behalf, but fearing the beating her mother might receive, Kakenya spoke for herself. She told her father that she wanted him to delay her marriage so that she could finish high school. She agreed to go through with the cutting ceremony if he would guarantee that she could finish school. If not, she threatened to run away and remain uncut. An uncut girl in his family would bring unbearable shame to her father, making him a subject of ridicule in the village. To everyone's surprise, he accepted her terms. Kakenya went through with the circumcision ritual, trading a piece of her body for the right to go to high school.

When her graduation approached, she knew she needed to make another deal. By this time, though, her father had become ill and was no longer in a position to make decisions for the family. "So, according to our custom," Kakenya explains, "all the men his age were now my father. I went to them one by one."

There is a Masai tradition that someone who visits before sunrise will bring good news, and they mustn't be told no. So each morning while it was still dark, Kakenya walked to the homes of each of the village elders and asked for their blessing for her to attend college in America.

When all of the elders had agreed, the people of Enoosaen sold some of their cows and pooled money to buy Kakenya a plane ticket to the United States. For the first time, a girl from Kakenya's village would go to college. She promised that she would return and bring the benefits of her education home to Enoosaen.

Vital Voices' partners at the Nike Foundation, who were engaged in developing the Girl Effect Campaign, an advocacy effort to drive development dollars towards investments in girls around the world, told me about Kakenya's incredible journey. I met her myself in 2006. By then, this young woman from a Masai village had received her MA and was a dissertation away from completing a PhD at the University of Pittsburgh.

Kakenya told me that she dreamed of providing opportunities for the girls in Enoosaen. By letting her attend school, her community had given her the opportunity to create her own future, to follow her dream. It was an investment she was determined to repay. "I vowed the day I left home that one day I would come back and . . . help more girls in my community go to school." She knew that if they were able to get a quality education and were encouraged to stay in school, their futures could be limitless.

"One hundred million girls are expected to become child brides in the next decade. But I see a different future for them," Kakenya tells me. "I see smiling faces full of energy and passion—ready to change their society for better."

In 2008 Vital Voices honored Kakenya with our Rising Voices Award. We chose her not only for her courage, her accomplishments, and the path she had blazed but also for the extraordinary dream she held onto for the future. It wasn't a dream for herself. It was a dream for her community and our world. That summer, I traveled to Enoosaen to witness the groundbreaking of the Kakenya Center for Excellence, the very first residential girls' primary school in her village. As we approached the village, after a four-hour drive across rough terrain into the heart of the Masai territory, I noticed men and women carrying chairs on their backs and on bicycles.

I soon found out they were bringing the chairs to the groundbreaking ceremony. The women cooked a feast, the children danced, and it seemed like every man in the village told me that he was Kakenya's brother or cousin or related to her in some way. The pride her community took in her achievements was as striking as the accomplishments themselves. Kakenya had pulled off something extraordinary, successfully and respectfully overcoming generations of tradition. Not only had she created an environment to nurture girls and grow leaders, she brought along a community of champions who see that educating girls can benefit everyone.

In May 2009 thirty-two girls were enrolled in the first class of the Kakenya Center for Excellence. Each year since then has seen thirty more. In 2011 Kakenya completed her PhD and returned to Kenya, where she can spend more time with the girls in the village and can begin to replicate the model of the Kakenya Center for Excellence in other parts of the country.

Kakenya did ultimately get married, but as she explains, "it was to a man *I* chose," a Kenyan from the Kikuyu tribe, whom she met at university. Armed with her PhD and busy with her own young family, Kakenya could have made Enoosaen a distant memory. She could have built her life in the United States, but she did not want the story to end with her success: she felt compelled to share her success with others.

Since Kakenya was a little girl dreaming of becoming a teacher, she has believed that *every child—it doesn't matter where they are—every child has a dream.* As of 2011 ninety girls were enrolled in her school. Kakenya hopes this is just the beginning for each of them. "I see them empowered and with proper education," she says. "I see them as senior executives in big companies, owning their own businesses, heading government ministries, and championing the rights for humanity. I want them to have dreams, dreams bigger than mine."

JAYA ARUNACHALAM
India

"A wave of change will not come from one person—it will come from a movement of thousands of empowered women."

Growing up, Jaya Arunachalam believed that the way to make change on a large scale was by serving in the government; so she got a good education, volunteered for the Indian National Congress Party, and set her sights on becoming a political leader. However, she soon realized that the real transformation of India had to come from the people themselves. In particular, Jaya was compelled by the situation of poor women in her country. She was convinced that India could never reach its full potential if it did not utilize half its natural resources—its women.

Jaya told me, when she and I met during one of my first trips to India, "the low socioeconomic status of women in India is our greatest barrier to development." Of the estimated 350–400 million people who live below the absolute poverty line, a majority are women.[10] And of the estimated eight million children between the ages of six and fourteen in India who are not in school, a majority are girls.[11] With low status in society and a lack of education, women are susceptible to domestic violence, trafficking, and HIV/AIDS. Undoubtedly, women's lack of information about the disease and how to prevent it, as well as their lack of decision-making power in sexual matters, compounds their vulnerability. Jaya began working to promote collective action among the poorest of poor women, motivating them to begin visualizing a better future for themselves and their children.

Around the same time the women's movement was picking up in the West, Jaya sought to empower Indian women economically through microfinance. "Many microfinance programs begin and end with the idea that if you give a poor woman a very small loan to start and build a small business, not only will she be able to help support her family, but she will repay the loan. At WWF [Working Women's Forum], we believe that increasing a family's income alone will not pull a woman out of poverty. Poverty is about the lack of access to resources, education, and rights." From its founding, WWF has stood for the principle that in order for real socioeconomic change to occur, women need to be empowered both economically and as active citizens—to understand their value in society and their rights.

Jaya used case studies to teach women about the impact of educating their children and the importance of health care. She disseminated information to help women lobby government officials on issues that affect their lives. And recognizing that no single organization could drive lasting change on its own, she assembled a network of advocates to work collectively for social, political, and economic progress. Soon Jaya found herself at the center of India's "silent revolution," a movement to empower the poorest of the poor.

Since 1978 the Working Women's Forum has empowered nearly a million poor women spread throughout 3,000 villages and 1,600 slums across India. These women are able to decide the number of children they want to have, to earn income to help support their families, and to understand and fight for their legal, political, labor, and housing rights. Through street marches and mass meetings, they draw public attention to their concerns.

Many of Jaya's network leaders make even greater change by representing their villages on local government councils known as Panchayats. Over a million women hold locally elected positions on Panchayats, the largest political representation of women in the world. The 2011 World Development Report on Gender noted that women's strong representation on Panchayats—where they hold 33 percent of seats in most regions of India—has led to greater development in infrastructure like roads, clean water, and education, and less government corruption and waste.[12]

Jaya understands that once you empower a woman, you have changed her forever. When the tsunami hit the southern coast of India in December 2004, many of the fisherwomen who were part of her network lost their livelihoods. She traveled to the south to console them, to see the destruction, and to help them rebuild. Because they were empowered, these women knew they had a network of support behind them, and even though they had lost everything, they had not lost their self-confidence. Jaya supported more than two thousand fisherwomen by providing food, clothing, and financial support to rebuild their businesses and their lives and continue to support their families. She believes strongly in her driving force: *set an example; lead from the front.*

SAMAR MINALLAH KHAN
Pakistan

"When it comes to women's rights or human rights, in Pakistan there is a kind of a culture of silence. It was very important that some sort of a movement based on media should somehow start that would challenge the mindset or that would help in breaking the silence."

As an activist and filmmaker, Samar Minallah Khan is making daring moves to transform culture. For over twenty years, she has fought for human rights in Pakistan, focusing on sanctioned acts of violence against women and girls. With film and outreach, Samar has amplified women's voices, empowered male heroes and advocates, and shined a spotlight on unseen human rights abuses throughout the country.

For Samar the seeds of leadership were planted early on. Growing up in Pakistan's North-West Frontier Province, she was close to her father, who believed in the importance of education and encouraged Samar to pursue her dreams. Although he passed away when Samar was just thirteen years old, his progressive ideals left an indelible impact, providing her with opportunities that were denied to so many of the girls she had grown up with. Indeed Samar did follow her dreams, and traveled all the way to Cambridge University to earn a degree in social anthropology and development. When she returned home to Pakistan, however, she saw her country and community through new eyes. As she reconnected with old friends and classmates, Samar understood the impact her father had made on the direction of her life. Educated and empowered, Samar enjoyed independence and freedom of choice, while many of her female peers lacked agency and suffered from violence at home. For Samar it felt as if her culture perceived individuals differently according to their gender: boys were valued as individuals, and girls were considered mere symbols of honor. This devastating realization motivated Samar to act. Recognizing the opportunities her father had brought her, she set out to encourage progressive values, challenge discriminatory cultural practices, and promote the equality of men and women in Pakistan.

Leaders like Samar are truly needed in a country such as Pakistan where the rights of women and girls remain unrealized. Estimates are that three women are sacrificed to honor-killings in Pakistan each day and that 80 percent of all adult women experience physical abuse from an intimate partner. The country is a source and destination for the global sex trafficking trade, forced or child marriage, acid burning, and domestic violence. Additionally, many Pakistani communities engage in the practice of Swara or Vanni, a thousand-year-old tradition that defines women and girls as peace offerings. The practice of Swara occurs when one family clan offers another family clan one of its female members in order to restore honor or settle a dispute. The new family clan then determines the fate of the woman or girl: sometimes she is forced to marry into the clan. Sometimes she is killed.

In an effort to combat these practices and build a different kind of culture, Samar founded the nonprofit organization Ethnomedia. Through the development of original media content, advocacy, and outreach, Samar hoped to accurately represent the perspectives, positions, and priorities of women, while shining a spotlight on harmful cultural barriers to their full access to human rights. As Samar began her work with Ethnomedia, she made an important observation. Many of the men in her community had a negative impression of nonprofits; they felt these organizations espoused a critical view of all men, regardless of their actions or beliefs. In recognition of these impressions and with her father's legacy in mind, Samar made strategic efforts to involve men in her organization's work. As Samar develops media content, she highlights male community members who support women's rights, and she solicits men's participation as advocates for her cause. Today, Samar believes that building future generations of gender-sensitive fathers is an integral part of her work.

Over the past two decades, Ethnomedia has been incredibly active. Through this organization Samar has created electronic media, publications, news features, documentary films, television programs, and music videos—effectively disseminating information on violence against women to researchers, civil society leaders, policy makers, and the greater public. Additionally, the organization has launched outreach campaigns to promote democracy, combat violence against women, and shine a spotlight on the plight of women in conflict. Perhaps most notably, Samar's work with Ethnomedia has been successful in combating the practice of Swara. After collecting a significant body of research and documenting the impact of Swara on Pakistani women and their families, Samar challenged this custom by engaging Islamic scholars, politicians, and feudal lords in discussion. In a bold and innovative effort to draw attention to the practice, Samar even convinced truck and rickshaw owners to paint slogans against Swara on their vehicles, such as "Giving away little girls as compensation is not only inhuman but also un-Islamic." And in 2006 Samar succeeded in bringing her fight against Swara all the way to Pakistan's Supreme Court. Resulting from Samar's continued efforts, the court passed a benchmark decision to penalize the act of "offering and accepting by way of compensation any child, or woman against her free will" in June of that year.

Although Samar's work has brought risk to her personal safety, she shows no signs of backing down. In fact when

Samar reflects on the success of her career, she recalls a time when her son, at age eleven, confronted her about the threats against her life. Looking earnestly at his mother, Samar's son declared that he would continue her work if anything ever happened to her. To date, Samar considers this moment one of the most rewarding experiences of her career; in this moment Samar's son showed her that the legacy of her father will live on in her family and in her community. Samar's efforts to bring opportunities to others demonstrate the power of paying it forward.

LEADERSHIP IS A JOURNEY, NOT A DESTINATION

INTRODUCED BY SALLY FIELD

Actress, Activist, and Vital Voices Board Member

SEVENTEEN YEARS AGO, I TOO TRAVELED TO BEIJING where I attended and participated in the historic UN Fourth World Conference on Women. I did not know what I would see and certainly was unable to anticipate how deeply it would affect me. My journey was perhaps magnified because my twenty-three-year-old son, who was in his third year of college at the time, accompanied me. As a mother, I watched this "typical American young man" stand in awe, listening to the stories of the women, young and old, from across the globe as they revealed their profound struggle for what to him had seemed so elemental.

I could see and feel him react to the immediacy and importance of what was being illuminated and watched the impact it had on him. The right to an education, the right to proper health care, the right to speak out, the right to economic freedom, the right to live without fear of violation: women's rights, certainly, but more than that, human rights.

No one among us walked away the same.

I learned that where women remain illiterate, democratic institutions are more fragile and the environment less well managed, and that investing in girls' education goes hand-in-hand with economic opportunity. Where women are empowered, they transform not only their own lives but the lives of their families and communities as well.

I realized how important it was for me as a woman in this global family, and as a mother of three sons, to find a way to join in this effort anyway I could. In the years that have followed, the leadership of pioneering women has brought this call for equality out from the darkness. These brave women have inspired the local council member, the social enterprise entrepreneur, and the civil society organizer. The women I have come to know in my time with Vital Voices have a unique and powerful ability to lead in a collaborative way that urges whole communities forward to change—closer to peace, closer to prosperity, closer to realizing their potential.

The challenges of today are tremendous, and the progress is tenuous if it's not reinforced and expanded. We—all of us—must move forward with the same sense of purpose and possibility that guides the leaders you have met in the pages of this book. In Beijing, for me, the silence was broken and the work has just begun. Please join that fight to create a lasting legacy for the power of voice in action.

O
N Saturday, November 13, 2010, Aung San Suu Kyi was released after having spent fifteen of the previous twenty-one years under house arrest. Over a thousand Burmese admirers and members of the international press gathered outside the gates of her home. As she walked towards them, crowds cheered, monks chanted, and children danced—and thousands more around the world rejoiced.

A week before Aung San Suu Kyi's release, the military regime had held the first elections in twenty years. Suu's party, the National League for Democracy (NLD), had refused to participate, calling the process a sham. Many speculated that releasing "the lady," though her sentence had been served, was just a ploy for the government to seek international legitimacy and to open discussions with the West on the sanctions that had crippled the Burmese economy.

Upon her release, Aung San Suu Kyi spoke out, asking the international community to look closely at the November 7 elections. Daw Suu had occasionally been set free in past years, only to be returned to house arrest. Now, in the days and weeks that followed, the world wondered whether that would be the case again, or whether the junta was genuinely interested in a thawing of relations.

At Vital Voices, we were determined to do whatever we could to support and pay tribute to her courageous struggle for democracy. We decided to honor Daw Suu with our Global Trailblazer Award, which would be presented by Secretary of State Hillary Clinton at the Kennedy Center in Washington, D.C., in April 2011. We knew that if Daw Suu left Burma, she might never be allowed to return. Instead,

I would travel to meet with her, accompanied by Aaron Kisner, Vital Voices' creative director. We wanted to discuss how Vital Voices could support her, and to record a video message to spread her words to a wider audience.

Our adventure took months of preparation and the help of a network of individuals who have dedicated their lives to the Burmese people. We were acutely aware that many journalists and even world leaders, like former British prime minister Gordon Brown, had been denied entry to Burma in the past, some landing at the airport in Yangon only to be turned away. But we were lucky. Aaron and I slipped through.

At the time, Burma had very little connection with the outside world. International cell phones didn't work, which made it difficult to link up with our local contact. To coordinate our meeting, we had to keep moving around the city, making calls from makeshift telephone operators who set up small shops on the street. Though Burma is almost exclusively a cash economy, there weren't ATM machines, which made it nearly impossible to access funds. And with so few Westerners in the city, we could pass as tourists for only so long. By the end of the first evening, we accepted the fact that we were being followed by a "minder."

On the morning of March 2, we took a taxi to the Shwedagon Pagoda, the site of Daw Suu's famous 1988 speech that launched her political journey. It was a holiday in Burma, commemorating exactly forty-nine years since the 1962 coup d'état that had established the army's political dominance—an eerie day to be meeting with the country's most prominent voice for democracy.

We ducked into a second taxi. The driver seemed nervous when I gave him the address for the NLD headquarters. We weren't far away, but as we rolled along the numbers on the buildings were going in the wrong direction, and I wondered if he was planning to deliver us to the police instead. After a roundabout route, we arrived at what looked like a vacant building: number 97B. I noticed that the driver's hands were shaking on the wheel. We got out quickly so that he would not be exposed and harassed, sidestepped some detritus, and entered. I felt like I could breathe for the first time since we entered Burma.

Inside the walls of the NLD headquarters, Daw Suu's office was quiet, as it was a national holiday. On her desk were old photos of her father, the revolutionary hero General Aung San; a collection of letters from supporters around the world; a decades-old Apple computer collecting dust; and stacks of international studies and reports.

Without fanfare, Daw Suu walked in. She wore a dainty pink blouse, fresh flowers tied back in her hair, and a traditional sarong. She looked more beautiful in person—yet fierce—than in any photograph I had seen. I had expected her to be formal, but she immediately put me at ease with mothering grace, humility, and surprising flashes of humor. There were times when we were speaking that I forgot where we were. She gave the impression of being in complete control.

Though she had endured great sacrifices for more than twenty years, she told me that she bears no personal resentment towards the junta. She admitted that sometimes she gets frustrated, but she quickly counters that frustration with hope. She loves the energy of young people and plans to travel the world one day to speak to students.

Sharing an hour with Aung San Suu Kyi was an extraordinary experience. Her story had captivated me since I first heard her speak via video at the UN conference in Beijing, seventeen years before. Yet in all that time she had been more of an icon to me than an actual person—an exquisite portrait of courage on a poster, not the frank and funny woman with whom I sat in an unassuming office in Yangon.

I asked her if she ever felt it was a burden to be held up as an icon. She said she didn't think of herself that way; that she was just a woman doing a job. It was astonishing to consider the sacrifices she has made in the name of that "job," even as she drew strength from the certainty she stood for something larger than herself. Though she never set out to be a figurehead, she was willing to serve as one if it was "useful."

We spoke about women throughout the world who struggle on the front lines of change. She asked me to give a message to the women I encounter: She does not want them to lose hope; this is the test for leaders; one must have the strength to stay the course. We spoke about the Arab Spring and how true and sustainable change comes about.

As we left the NLD offices, I took one last look at her humble headquarters, wondering how different Burma might have been with Aung San Suu Kyi at the helm. The military rulers may have the power of coercion, but Aung San Suu Kyi holds the power of the people's hearts, giving them hope when they have little else.

Being with her felt like coming full circle on this leadership journey, a journey during which I have frequently looked to her image for inspiration. I never could have imagined, when I set off for Beijing in the summer of 1995, that the women I would encounter there would alter my life's trajectory. The leadership lessons revealed by their stories—lessons that have been reinforced by the transformational women I've encountered since—fueled my conviction that a new paradigm of leadership is at hand. This is a paradigm exemplified by women but not exclusive to women. That meeting with Aung San Suu Kyi reminded me that we may never be presented with the perfect formula or situation to lead change; we must be pragmatic and seize opportunities as they arise. She made me realize that these lessons and this model needed to be shared more broadly, because it is a model anyone can follow—and one our world desperately needs right now.

• • •

The contemporary challenges of our world call for a new paradigm of leadership. If we want to see transformational change take hold, we need to recognize the power of possibility that this model represents, and our role in bringing it to bear.

An ever more interconnected world needs participatory leaders.
A world with a widening rich-poor divide needs inclusive, collaborative leaders.

A world scarred by misunderstanding and mistrust among peoples, religions, and cultures needs leaders who are rooted in their communities yet determined also to build bridges with others.

A world confronted with urgent challenges—some long-standing, others fast-emerging—needs innovative leaders who will reinvest the benefits of their experience in rising generations.

Most important, a world in constant flux needs leaders who will step up *now*, regardless of their current status, position, or means.

The women who have taught us about leadership didn't wait. They didn't delay taking action to seek out funding, training, experience, or the invitation or recognition of others. They understood that there is no perfect moment for leadership to begin. They rose from wherever they were, with what resources they had, to challenge the status quo however they could.

Their stories remind us that no one among us is powerless to make an impact; that even in environments which actively resist or deny their rights, women can rise as defenders of political reform, economic opportunity, and human development. Moreover, their examples teach us that leadership is not a destination one can aspire to reach only after having achieved many other things; in fact it is not a destination at all. It is a choice we make anew each day, recognizing that the most important step in a leader's journey is always the one we are just about to take.

Anyone can make a difference.

Opportunity to make change is all around us, and we are never too young or inexperienced to try. Often, in fact, young people are the most perceptive in identifying such opportunities—and the least cynical about the prospects for success.

In the fall of 1999, for example, two high school newspaper reporters in Berkeley, California, Megan Greenwell and Iliana Montauk, heard about the tragic death of a young Indian woman from carbon monoxide poisoning. She lived in an apartment complex just a few blocks from their school and was about their age at the time of her death. Megan and Iliana started asking questions: *Where were her parents? Why wasn't she in school?* They suspected that there was more to the story than what they had read in the local news.

They conducted interviews with other students in the neighborhood, with residents in the building complex, and with members of the local South Asian community. The high schoolers discovered that the girl had been in the United States illegally, smuggled in as part of a human trafficking ring and forced into servitude. The girls broke the story in their school newspaper, the *Berkeley High Jacket*, prompting the arrest of a prominent local landlord, Lakireddy Bali Reddy, and ultimately the collapse of a powerful crime ring.[1]

An extraordinary example, yes, but this story is not as rare as one might think. All over the world, there are girls and young women who are leading change. In 2008 ten-year-old Najood Ali, a Yemeni girl from an impoverished and illiterate family, was married to a thirty-year-old deliveryman. Under Yemen's civil status law, this was perfectly legal.

Over the first few months of their marriage, Najood endured repeated rapes and beatings—until one day, she found the courage to take her destiny into her own hands. She escaped from the house and took a taxi to the local courthouse. There she stunned everyone by submitting a request for a divorce. No young girl had ever stood up for herself so publicly, and Najood quickly gained the attention of the national press. Shada Nasser, the first female lawyer in Yemen, took on her case. They went to trial, and a judge granted Najood a divorce and then ordered the arrests of her husband and father.

Najood's story quickly spread around the world, spurring new awareness about child marriage—which affects more than ten million girls under eighteen worldwide each year[2]—and igniting a global campaign to end the practice. Later that year, the Yemeni Parliament created a law that set the minimum marriage age at seventeen. And in 2011 the Elders—a group of former heads of state and world leaders—launched the "Girls Not Brides" campaign to end child marriage within a generation.[3] Archbishop Desmond Tutu declared the practice "slavery" and vowed to devote to this global cause the same energy, passion, and commitment he had brought to ending apartheid.

Also in 2011, inspired by a shared belief in young women and girls as an important constituency for change, Vital Voices joined Ann Inc., the parent company of Ann Taylor and Loft clothing stores, to launch the ANNpower Initiative. The program identifies American girls of high school age who demonstrate—like Megan, Iliana, and Najood—the potential to catalyze positive change in their communities and our world. Each year a group of fifty girls receives leadership training from many of the extraordinary women featured in this book, as well as a vibrant support network to help them create their first ripples of change.

Big change often begins with small endeavors.
In the run-up to the 1975 United Nations First World Conference on Women, a Kenyan delegate named Wangari Maathai traveled around her native country, speaking with women about the challenges they faced in their everyday lives. They told her of poverty and a lack of clean drinking water, nutritious food, and firewood.

Wangari—who had left Kenya in 1960 to complete her studies in the United States—was struck by the differences between the life she had led growing up in the 1940s and 1950s and the realities Kenyan women faced only fifteen years later. While her family had never been wealthy, they had never considered themselves poor. They lived off the land. There had always been enough food, clean drinking water, and wood for fires.

However, the 1970s brought deforestation and devegetation practices—implemented to prepare land for commercial crops—which had eroded the soil. Industrial development disrupted the old patterns of life in rural Kenya, leaving the people without the natural resources they needed to sustain themselves. Often it was women who were the hardest hit. They were the ones responsible for fetching water and firewood; and as resources became scarce, they had to venture out farther and farther every day in order to support their families.

Wangari came up with a simple plan. She planted trees, indigenous trees. Her idea caught on and spread. Within just twenty years, with few resources and little technology, she had changed the face of Kenya. As of 2012 the Greenbelt Movement that she started has planted more than forty million trees, and changed an untold number of lives for the better—an achievement that garnered her the 2004 Nobel Prize in Peace.

Leadership calls for patience, and for commitment to stay the course.

In 2011 Dr. Maathai passed away from complications related to ovarian cancer. A few years earlier, I had the opportunity to meet her and ask her what she felt was the most important attribute of a leader. She responded, "If you look at people like Mahatma Gandhi, or Indira Gandhi herself, these people have had a vision; have had a passion. They pursued that passion with a determination. They were patient because they knew that things don't happen overnight. But they were also persistent. They stayed with that idea, as long as they felt that 'this is it.'"

Sustainable change doesn't happen overnight. Social scientist Anders Ericsson's research in the early 1990s uncovered that it takes ten thousand hours of committed practice to be an expert at anything—whether it's playing a musical instrument or a sport, or leading in a profession. Similarly, creating real change will often take years of commitment. Guo Jianmei described the early days of her work for women's rights in China as "struggling uphill with a heavily loaded cart against a strong wind." Inez McCormack has spoken about how her work for peace and civil rights in Northern Ireland was "first demonized, but now has been lauded."

Leaders are defined, not defeated, by setbacks.
Almost every leader I've encountered has a story of a setback. Roshaneh Zafar of Pakistan believes that it was her original misstep—excluding men from her lending strategy—that equipped her with the knowledge she needed to make Kashf the huge success it is today. Sunitha Krishnan of India learned early on that passion was not enough to sustain her organization. Kakenya Ntaiya was so determined to change the lives of Masai girls that she underestimated the cultural barriers to new ideas; she needed to take two steps back to gain the trust of her community before she could take three steps forward to improve it.

What matters most is not the act of failing but how we pick ourselves up after we get knocked down, and what lessons we take away. Arianna Huffington wisely advised, "Don't be afraid to fail. Failure is not the opposite of success. It is a stepping stone *to* success." The power of these cause-driven leaders is rooted in self-awareness: clarity of purpose combined with a humility towards one's strengths and weaknesses.

Everyone has a platform from which to lead.
Beth Brooke, the global vice chair of Ernst & Young, has said that for her a real wake-up call came in 2003. Over dinner one night, her best female friend said very directly, "you don't do enough for women." Beth says she about died. She got upset and spouted off all the things she did for women

and complained that there was no way she could do more. "But I went home that night, thought about it, and realized she was right," recalls Beth. What her friend had meant was that as a top executive in a Fortune 500 firm, Beth had a platform. She could use that platform to drive change not only within the company but also in the outside world with government leaders, other top executives, and the media. "I wasn't using my bigger platform in any strategic way to help the cause of women more broadly. Yes, I was mentoring, shepherding, promoting, etc. And doing all that was expected of me. . . . But there was so much more influence I could be asserting if I used my platform thoughtfully—and in ways nobody would have expected, which of course makes it all the more powerful and impactful." For Beth it was a breakthrough moment on using the power of the platform as a real, authentic leader. And in the wake of the global financial crisis of 2008, Ernst & Young, with Beth's strong leadership, became one of the corporations best known for promoting the value of tapping women's potential to pull companies and countries out of recession, launching as it did a series of studies and discussions on the topic.

You needn't have a multinational corporation behind you to lead change. The girls in Berkeley, California, had only their network of parents, their teachers, and their school newspaper. Yet they leveraged the platform they had to build a broad base of support, and ultimately to attain a much larger platform. Everyone has a circle of influence that matters, no matter how small. Small ripples of change flow outward, and those circles of influence grow.

Opportunity is waiting to be seized.

Sometimes I wonder what my life's path would have been like if I hadn't made the journey to the Beijing women's conference when I was twenty-one. What if I had been deterred by the Chinese government's decision to deny me the conference visa? What if I hadn't taken that leap of faith? It is the risks we take that shape who we are, and the lessons we choose to learn from the experience that give us the confidence we need to confront each new challenge.

Leadership of the future begins with the framework that the women profiled here have brought to life:

- A driving force or sense of mission
- Strong roots in the community
- An ability to connect across lines that divide
- Bold ideas and bold action
- A resolve to pay it forward

But for all these commonalities, for each new leader the context, the challenges, and the strategies for success will be her own.

The lessons contained herein come directly from our distilled experience with women leaders around the world. These women humble and inspire us every day. They give new meaning and new credibility to the title "leader." Alone, each of them is extraordinary; together, they are transformational. Each one illuminates the art of the possible.

Leadership is about the decisions that you make and the actions that you take each day. The world is waiting. Leadership is a choice—and it starts with you.

SUSAN ANN DAVIS AND BOBBIE GREENE McCARTHY

Chair and Vice-Chair, Board of Directors,
Vital Voices

WE ARE GRATEFUL AND PROUD TO BE a part of Vital Voices as we search the globe for women leaders who we believe are poised to make a major impact. Our admiration for these pathfinders never lags as we invest in their potential to make real what they dare to dream for their communities, for our world.

Emerging from the darkest violence, *Sunitha Krishnan* determined to create a world in which human dignity is protected and life is never bought, traded, or discarded. Today, her sense of purpose fuels an offensive against human trafficking and slavery in India.

Maria Pacheco's unique understanding of local needs in Guatemala guides her as she transforms once intractable rural poverty into sustainable development by connecting indigenous communities to international markets.

Out of her commitment to an inclusive and lasting peace for Northern Ireland, *Inez McCormack* unites across lines that divide, around a shared vision for the future.

Extraordinary courage led *Rebecca Lolosoli* to speak out against injustice and establish a refuge for Kenyan survivors of violence who had been cast out of their families and communities.

Israeli citizens, one Arab and one Jewish, *Noha Khatieb* and *Liron Peleg-Hadomi*, are building a legacy of tolerance and understanding as a living example of imagined peace for the young peace-builders they mentor.

These women and countless others lead us all forward. In resistant societies and intolerant climates, they light the way. With calm conviction, they urge us toward the world they envision: free, fair, and filled with promise.

So what began as an idea, an aspiration to give a platform to anonymous heroines who raise others up, is now a catalyst for future leadership.

For the two of us, Vital Voices brings new passion and purpose to our lives. We feel truly blessed to share this journey—and this planet—with these remarkable women who represent the very best humanity has to offer.

ADDITIONAL INFORMATION ON THE WOMEN FEATURED IN *VITAL VOICES*

In this section, you can learn more about the women featured in this book or about their organizations.

Esraa Abdel Fattah

Egypt

Egyptian Democratic Academy (EDA)

http://egyda.org/blog/

Esraa received international recognition for sparking the 2011 revolution in Egypt due to her use of social networking, which garnered the attention of thousands of Egyptians. The Egyptian Democratic Academy (EDA) is a youth organization established by a group of human rights and democracy activists working to promote the values of democracy, human rights, and political participation.

Hawa Abdi

Somalia

Hawa Abdi Hospital and Hawa Abdi Foundation

http://www.dhaf.org/

Dr. Abdi, a medical doctor by training, and Amina and Deqo Mohamed, her two daughters, who are also doctors, run a refugee camp that provides shelter, education, and medical attention to approximately 78,000 Somalis in a declared nonviolent safe haven outside war-torn Mogadishu. The Hawa Abdi Foundation was one of the first NGOs to open in Somalia, and aims to provide quality health care, education for local nurses and midwives, and aid for the empowerment of women in their communities. For further reading, see the forthcoming book, *Keeping Hope Alive*, by Dr. Hawa Abdi and Sarah J. Robbins (publication date of May 2013).

Hafsat Abiola

Nigeria

Kudirat Initiative for Democracy (KIND)
www.kind.org
Hafsat launched KIND in Nigeria to promote women's full participation in society through training and advocacy. KIND trains young women to take responsibility for their personal and professional lives and to participate in politics and decision-making at the community and national levels.

Afnan Al Zayani

Bahrain

Al Zayani Commercial Services; Bahrain Business Women's Society (BBWS)
http://www.bahrainbusinesswomen.com/
http://www.menabwn.org/
Afnan is a CEO, author, and television show host and is head of the Bahrain Business Women's Society (BBWS), which promotes the role of women, especially businesswomen, in all commercial and economic activities, and supports women in all fields that would show their participation on the local, Gulf, and international scales. She also leads the Middle East North Africa Businesswomen's Network.

Lubna Al-Kazi

Kuwait

Professor, Kuwait University, and Former Head, Kuwaiti Women's Social and Cultural Society

Lubna is a professor of sociology and key advocate for women's equality in Kuwait, whose activism was crucial to the 2005 passage of the law granting Kuwaiti women the right to vote and run for office. In 1991, Lubna led the Kuwaiti Women's Social and Cultural Society, the premier women's rights group in Kuwait.

Laura Alonso

Argentina

Member of Congress, Argentina

http://www.poderciudadano.org.ar/

Laura left her role as executive director of Poder Ciudadano (Citizen Power), a renowned watchdog group that promoted transparency and fought corruption, to become a member of Congress for the PRO Party. She has taken steps to publicly and personally promote transparency as her own personal mission from within the government.

Jaya Arunachalam

India

Working Women's Forum (WWF)

http://www.workingwomensforum.org

As president of WWF, Jaya works to provide economic stability for rural women workers in India through training, provision of resources, and advocacy to bring their struggles and needs to the public. The mission of WWF is to reduce poverty and strengthen the economic, social, and cultural status of poor working women through microcredit, training, social mobilization, and other interventions to poor women.

Panmela Castro

Brazil

Anarkia Graffiti

http://www.anarkiaboladona.com/

Rede Nami

http://www.redenami.com/

Panmela, a classically trained artist, is a renowned graffiti artist in Rio de Janeiro, who uses her art to bring attention to issues related to women, such as domestic violence. She also created murals to publicize the landmark passage of the Maria da Penha Bill, which criminalized domestic violence in Brazil.

Rita Chaikin

Israel

Isha L'Isha—Haifa Feminist Center

http://www.isha.org.il/eng/

Rita works to eradicate human trafficking in Israel and has helped the government, law officials, and nongovernmental organizations better collaborate in identifying, assisting, and protecting victims, prosecuting traffickers, and educating the public.

Sohini Chakraborty

India

Kolkata Sanved

http://kolkatasanved.org/

Sohini travels across India using dance as a form of expression and healing to rehabilitate children who are victims of human trafficking. Kolkata Sanved works in rural and urban India, Bangladesh, and Nepal to establish dance movement as an alternative approach to recovery and healing for the psychosocial rehabilitation of victims of violence and trafficking, mental health patients, women and children suffering from HIV/AIDS, domestic workers, railway platform children, and mainstream school children. Kolkata Sanved has performed and conducted workshops worldwide.

Anabella de Leon

Guatemala

Member of Congress, Third National Secretary of the Patriotic Party
Anabella has spent her life fighting corruption and promoting transparency despite personal risk. She is known for advocating on behalf of indigenous communities in Guatemala, and participated in the Guatemalan Peace Accords, which ended the civil war that plagued the country for decades.

Natalia Dmytruk

Ukraine

Sign Language Interpreter
Natalia received international attention in 2004 when working for state-run television for refusing to sign Viktor Yanukovych as the winner of the presidential elections because of the wide-known corruption and election rigging. She instead signed, "Everything you have heard so far is a lie. Yushchenko is our true president. Good-bye, for you will probably never see me here again."

Brigitte Dzogbenuku

Ghana

Mentoring Women Ghana
http://www.mwghana.org/home/index.php?option=com_
content&view=article&id=21&Itemid=8
Brigitte is a fitness and wellness expert who, after participating in the Fortune / State Department Global Women's Mentoring Partnership, started Sista Hoops, a mentoring program that integrates sports as a means for empowerment and self-confidence.

Andeisha Farid

Afghanistan

Afghan Child Education and Care Organization (AFCECO)
http://www.afceco.org/index.php/home
Andeisha runs ten orphanages in Afghanistan, where she not only provides homes for 450 children but promotes education and works to change public perceptions of these children in Kabul.

Oda Gasinzigwa

Rwanda

Gender Monitoring Officer, Rwanda
Oda works to create opportunities for women in Rwanda as well as research the inequalities that exist. She was an advocate for ensuring that women's voices were heard during the rebuilding of the country following the civil war.

Leymah Gbowee

Liberia

Women Peace and Security Network Africa
http://www.wipsen-africa.org/wipsen/
Leymah is executive director of Women Peace and Security Network Africa and was the 2011 recipient of the Nobel Peace Prize for her work organizing women across ethnic and cultural lines to peace building following Liberia's devastating civil war, including her work on the Truth and Reconciliation Committee.

Asha Hagi Elmi

Somalia

Save Somali Women and Children (SSWC)
Asha works to promote a peaceful Somalia through the support and empowerment of women. Asha is known for creating the Sixth

Clan, a clan of women that could be included in the traditional Five Clan structure of power in Somalia. Asha founded Save Somali Women and Children, a nonprofit organization based in Mogadishu with a presence across the country, to advocate for the formal recognition of Somali women's individual identities and rights.

Latifa Jbabdi

Morocco

Women's Action Union (UAF)
http://www.uaf.ma/an/file.php
Latifa is a women's rights activist in Morocco who works for women's equality in Morocco. She was critical in the monumental change to the Family Code in 2004.

Guo Jianmei

China

Center for Women's Law & Legal Service
http://www.woman-legalaid.org.cn/#
Guo is a lawyer and human rights activist who has also provided legal aid to women through her organization and has been instrumental in helping the government rewrite laws that protect women. She created the China NGO Legal Aid Cooperative Group and the China Women's Legal Aid Network, bringing together advocates, lawyers, hospitals, sociologists, public officials, courts, schools, journalists, NGOs, and psychologists in twenty-eight provinces across China.

Tawakkul Karman

Yemen

Women Journalists Without Chains
http://womenpress.org/index.php?lng=english

Tawakkul is founder of Women Journalists Without Chains and was the 2011 recipient of the Nobel Peace Prize for her work as a journalist and human rights activist, and her emerging leadership during the Yemen protests, which temporarily put her in prison.

Noha Khatieb

Israel

Director of Civil and Multicultural Education, Israel Ministry of Education
Noha has worked for over twenty years to create understanding between Israeli Jews and Israeli Arabs through integrated Hand in Hand Schools in Israel and through creating curriculum for Jewish and Arab schools for Israel's Ministry of Education.

Sunitha Krishnan

India

Prajwala
http://www.prajwalaindia.com
Sunitha founded Prajwala in Hyderabad to rescue women from brothels and provide education to their children. Prajwala educates 5,000 children through seventeen schools and, as of December 2011, had rescued more than 6,436 women and children from prostitution.

Rebecca Lolosoli

Kenya

Umoja Women's Village
http://www.umojawomen.org/
Fed up with the violence that women faced in her Samburu community, Rebecca created a safe-haven village for women in Northern Kenya, which promotes nonviolence and works to create

economic opportunities for the residents through the traditional practice of beading.

Mukhtaran Mai

Pakistan

Human Rights Activist
Women's Welfare Organization
http://www.mukhtarmai.org/
Mukhtaran received international acclaim for suing men who had raped her, an act commanded by village elders in response to acts by her brother. Books and movies have been created telling her story, such as the book *In the Name of Honor: A Memoir*. She used the money she received from her court case to build schools in her village.

Somaly Mam

Cambodia

Somaly Mam Foundation; Agir Pour les Femmes en Situation Précaire (AFESIP)
http://www.somaly.org/about-smf/somaly-mam
http://www.afesip.org/
Somaly used her dark past of being sold into sex slavery as a young girl to make it her personal mission to rescue and rehabilitate girls who have met the same fate. For further reading, see Somaly's book, *The Road of Lost Innocence: The True Story of a Cambodian Heroine.*

Inez McCormack

Northern Ireland

Participation and the Practice of Rights Project
http://www.pprproject.org/

Inez is a leading peace activist in Northern Ireland who participated in the creation of the 1998 Good Friday peace accords. Participation and the Practice of Rights (PPR) supports disadvantaged groups to assert their right to participate in social and economic decisions which affect their lives. PPR currently works on issues including mental health, adequate housing, regeneration, and the right to play with groups across the island of Ireland.

Samar Minallah Khan

Pakistan
Ethnomedia
http://www.ethnomedia.pk/
Samar is a documentary filmmaker, journalist, human rights activist, and anthropologist. She completed a documentary on *Swara*—the practice wherein girls are given as compensation to end disputes—which led to the practice being made illegal in 2004. Samar runs Ethnomedia, a nongovernmental media initiative bringing attention to culturally sanctioned forms of violence.

Chouchou Namegabe Dubuisson

Democratic Republic of Congo
South Kivu Women's Media Association (AFEM)
http://www.afemsk.blogspot.com/
Chouchou is a journalist and radio show host who has used her influence to bring to light the human rights atrocities that plague war-torn Congo. With the South Kivu Women's Media Association (AFEM), she has brought women's stories to the public and has brought international attention to the casualties of war in her country.

Kakenya Ntaiya

Kenya
Kakenya's Center for Excellence

http://kakenyasdream.org/academy.html
After fighting for the continuation of her own education in her Masai village of Enoosaen and receiving her PhD in education, Kakenya returned to her home to create a school for girls in the hope that no girl will have to fight for her education again.

Carmelita Gopez Nuqui

The Philippines
Development Action for Women Network (DAWN)
http://www.dawnphil.org/milestones.htm
Carmelita founded DAWN to bring attention to the issue of human trafficking and to advocate for the reduction in tourist visas the Philippines grants to Japan, after she realized that they were being used to traffick women.

Maria Pacheco

Guatemala
Kiej de los Bosques
http://www.kiejdelosbosques.com/index.html
Maria works to connect indigenous communities in Guatemala and other countries in Latin America to markets in order to promote economic independence and maintain traditional indigenous culture. She also started the Central American Chapter of Vital Voices.

Liron Peleg-Hadomi

Israel
Coordinator, Lead Haifa
Liron is a community social worker and has worked with NGOs committed to strengthening relations between Jews and Arabs in Israel. She is a coordinator of Lead Haifa and engages with leaders from the private sector, civil society, and the Haifa municipality on issues of personal development, joint learning, and social change.

Marina Pisklakova

Russia

Center ANNA (National Center for the Prevention of Violence)
http://anna-center.ru/
As the first domestic violence hotline for women in Russia, Center ANNA (National Center for the Prevention of Violence) is an organization that is engaged in the prevention of various forms of violence against women at all levels. As of 2012, the network comprised more than 160 organizations. Center ANNA and its network of partners have helped more than 200,000 women.

Danielle Saint-Lot

Haiti

Femmes en Démocratie (FED)
http://fed.org.ht/
Danielle has dedicated her professional career to promoting women's rights and empowerment through a variety of outlets throughout Haiti. From supporting women political candidates to launching an initiative for Haitian women artisans, Danielle and FED are dedicated to finding avenues for prosperity for women in Haiti.

Rosana Schaack

Liberia
THINK
http://www.thinkliberia.com/
Rosana founded Touching Humanity in Need of Kindness (THINK) in April 2003 to provide grassroots support for peace processes in Liberia. In October 2003 she opened THINK Rehabilitation Home, which provides therapy, education, and

support to girls who were soldiers, survivors of trafficking, victims of violence, sex workers, or separated from their families because of war.

Mu Sochua

Cambodia

Member of Cambodian Parliament
http://musochua.org/
Sochua has used her position as a member of Cambodia's Parliament to bring to light human rights abuses and issues pertaining to women throughout her country.

Adimaimalaga Tafuna'i

Samoa

Women in Business Development, Inc. (WIBDI)
http://www.womeninbusiness.ws/
Adi co-founded Women in Business Development, Inc. (WIBDI) in 1991 to address economic challenges facing rural Samoan women. In addition, she developed WIBDI's relationship with The Body Shop, where members now sell organic virgin coconut oil. She serves as executive director of WIBDI, where she runs programs on microfinance and financial literacy.

Anel Townsend Diez-Canseco

Peru

Former member of Congress, Minister of Women's Affairs and Social Development
Anel, once a journalist, jumped into politics in 1995 to combat corruption and promote women's participation in the political process. She continues to promote gender equality and public transparency in Peru and Latin America and serves as an

advisor and consultant for various organizations, such as the Inter-American Development Bank, the Inter-American Commission of Women of the Organization of American States, and the World Bank.

Kah Walla

Cameroon
STRATEGIES!
http://www.kahwalla.com
Kah is an entrepreneur and the CEO of her own consulting firm, STRATEGIES. Since 2007 she has held a city council position; she ran for president of Cameroon in 2011 on the platform of fighting corruption and promoting the needs of the marginalized populations in Cameroon.

Roshaneh Zafar

Pakistan
Kashf Foundation
http://www.kashf.org/site_files/default.asp
Roshaneh works to economically empower rural Pakistani women through microcredit loans and job creation by providing employment for women at her bank, which distributes the loans. Kashf Foundation (meaning miracle or revelation, that is, a process of self-discovery) began in 1996 and was the first microfinance institution targeting only women from low-income communities; it was also the first microfinance institution to charge a sustainable price for its services.

NOTES

Introduction

1. O'Connor, Sarah. "Iceland Calls in Women Bankers to Clean Up 'Young Men's Mess,'" *Financial Times*, Oct. 14, 2008. http://www .ft.com/intl/cms/s/0/6107e59c-9988-11dd-9d48-000077b07658 .html#axzz1gQtr7LMQ.

2. Lagarde, Christine. "Women, Power, and the Challenge of the Financial Crisis." *New York Times*, May 11, 2010. http://www.ny times.com/2010/05/11/opinion/11iht-edlagarde.html.

3. "Women: A Work Never Done," *The Economist Online*, Mar. 8, 2011. http://www.economist.com/blogs/dailychart/2011/03/women.

4. "The lion kings?" *The Economist Online*, Jan. 6, 2011. http://www.economist.com/node/17853324.

5. Lawson, Sandra, and Goldman Sachs. "Women Hold Up Half the Sky." Global Economics Paper No: 164, Mar. 4, 2008.

6. Summers, Lawrence H., and World Bank. "Investing in All the People: Educating Women in Developing Countries." EDI Seminar Paper No. 45, 1994.

7. Kent, Muhtar. "Who Will Drive the 21st Century Agenda? Women," Coca-Cola Company. http://www.thecoca-colacompany.com/dyna mic/leadershipviewpoints/2010/10/women-key-to-global-eco nomic-growth-kent-tells-yale-students.html.

8. *UNESCAP*. "Economic and Social Survey of Asia and the Pacific 2007: Surging Ahead in Uncertain Times," 2007, (103). http://www .unescap.org/survey2007/download/01_Survey_2007.pdf.

9. *UNICEF.* "The State of the World's Children 2011." Chapter 4: Investing in Adolescents. (74) http://www.unicef.org/sowc2011/pdfs/SOWC-2011-Main%20Report-chapter%204_12082010.pdf.

10. "The importance of sex." *The Economist*, Apr 12th, 2006. http://www.economist.com/node/6800723.

11. *United Nations Development Fund for Women,* "Investing in Women–Solving the Poverty Puzzle." 2007. http://www.womenfight poverty.org/docs/WorldPovertyDay2007_FactsAndFigures.pdf..

12. Rampell, Catherine. "Women Now a Majority in American Workplaces." *The New York Times.* Feb. 5, 2010. http://www.nytimes.com/2010/02/06/business/economy/06women.html.

13. *World Bank.* "Gender Action Plan: Gender Equality as Smart Economics." 2011. http://web.worldbank.org/WBSITE/EXTERNAL/TOPICS/EXTGENDER/0,,contentMDK:21983335~pagePK:2100 58~piPK:210062~theSitePK:336868,00.html.

14. *White House.* "United States National Action Plan on Women, Peace, and Security," Dec. 2011. http://www.whitehouse.gov/sites/default/files/email-files/US_National_Action_Plan_on_Women _Peace_and_Security.pdf.

15. Benschop, Marjolein. "Women's Rights to Land and Property," Commission on Sustainable Development, Apr. 2004. http://www.unhabitat.org/downloads/docs/1556_72513_CSDWomen.pdf.

16. *Women's Economic Opportunity Index* (New York: Economist Intelligence Unit Limited, 2010), 23.

   Women's Economic Opportunity Index (New York: Economist Intelligence Unit Limited, 2010), 23-24.

   Women's Economic Opportunities in the Formal Private Sector in Latin America and the Caribbean (Washington DC: The International Bank for Reconstruction and Development/The World Bank, 2010), 11.

   Rama Ramaswami et al., *Scaling up: Why Women-owned Businesses Can Recharge the Global Economy* (EYGM Limited, 2009), 14.

   Martin Valdivia, "Training or Technical Assistance? A Field Experiment to Learn What Works to Increase Managerial Capital for Female Microentrepreneurs." (Paper presented at the World Bank Conference on Female Entrepreneurship, Washington, DC, April 6, 2011), 47.

Kirrin Gill, et al., *Bridging the Gender Divide: How Technology Can Advance Women Economically* (Washington DC: The International Center for Research on Women, 2010), 2.

Kirrin Gill, et al., *Bridging the Gender Divide: How Technology Can Advance Women Economically* (Washington DC: The International Center for Research on Women, 2010), 3.

Women's Economic Opportunities in the Formal Private Sector in Latin America and the Caribbean (Washington DC: The International Bank for Reconstruction and Development/The World Bank, 2010), 11.

Sarah Gammage, et al., *Enhancing Women's Access to Markets: An Overview of Donor Programs and Best Practices* (Washington DC: USAID, 2005), 11.

Enhancing Women's Market Access and Promoting Pro-poor Growth, in *Promoting Pro-Poor Growth: Private Sector Development* (Paris: OECD, 2006), 67.

Donna J. Kelley, et al., *Global Entrepreneurship Monitor 2010 Report: Women Entrepreneurs Worldwide* (Babson College and the Global Entrepreneurship Research Association, 2011), 42.

Donna J. Kelley, et al., *Global Entrepreneur Monitor 2010 Report: Women Entrepreneurs Worldwide* (Babson College and the Global Entrepreneurship Research Association, 2011), 29.

Donna J. Kelley, et al., *Global Entrepreneur Monitor 2010 Report: Women Entrepreneurs Worldwide* (Babson College and the Global Entrepreneurship Research Association, 2011), 43.

Claudia Piras, "Chile Emprendedoras: Promoting Women in Dynamic Business," Presentation at the World Bank Conference on Female Entrepreneurship, Washington, DC, April 6, 2011.

Women's Economic Opportunities in the Formal Private Sector in Latin America and the Caribbean (Washington DC: The International Bank for Reconstruction and Development/The World Bank, 2010), 36-37.

Elaine Allen, et al., *Global Entrepreneurship Monitor 2007 Report on Women and Entrepreneurship* (Babson College and the Global Entrepreneurship Research Association, 2007), 9.

Women, Business and the Law: Measuring Legal Gender Parity for Entrepreneurs and Workers in 128 Economies (Washington DC: The International Bank for Reconstruction and Development/The World Bank, 2010), 5 and 8.

17. Katz, Jonathan. "The Business Case for Supply Chain Diversity." *Industry Week.* Nov. 16, 2011. http://www.industryweek.com/articles /the_business_case_for_supply_chain_diversity_26010.aspx?Show All=1.

18. Economist Intelligence Unit, Women's Economic Opportunity Index, 2010, page 13.

19. Bachelet, Michelle. "A Comprehensive Policy Agenda to End Violence Against Women: Prevention, Protection and Provision of Services Key." *UN Women.* Nov. 22, 2011. http://www.unwomen.org /2011/11/a-comprehensive-policy-agenda-to-end-violence-against -women/.

20. *United Nations Development Fund for Women.* "Violence Against Women—Facts and Figures," Nov. 2007. http://www.unifem.org /attachments/gender_issues/violence_against_women/facts_figures _violence_against_women_2007.pdf.

21. *United Nations Entity for Gender Equality and the Empowerment of Women.* "2011–2012 Progress of the World's Women: In Pursuit of Justice." http://progress.unwomen.org/pdfs/EN-Report -Progress.pdf.

Chapter 1

1. *US Department of State.* "Background Note: Burma." Aug. 3, 2011. http://www.state.gov/r/pa/ei/bgn/35910.htm.

2. *US Department of State.* "Background Note: Burma." Aug. 3, 2011. http://www.state.gov/r/pa/ei/bgn/35910.htm.

3. Sejersted, Francis. "Award Ceremony Speech." *Nobel Prize.* 1991. http://www.nobelprize.org/nobel_prizes/peace/laureates/1991/pre sentation-speech.html?print=1.

4. "Gendercide: The War on Baby Girls." *The Economist*. March 4, 2010. Accessed August 15, 2011. http://www.economist.com/node/156062 29?story_id=15606229&source=most_commented. "Tens of Millions of 'Missing' Girls." *CNN*. September 5, 2010. Accessed August 18, 2011. http://articles.cnn.com/2010-09-05/opinion/wudunn.wo men.oppression_1_baby-girls-sheryl-wudunn-girls-in-many-coun tries?_s=PM:OPINION.

5. "Hillary Clinton Urged to Skip China; Dole, Lugar Say Trip to Women's Conference Would Not Help U.S." *Washington Post*, Aug. 21, 1995.

6. Clinton, Hillary Rodham. *Living History*. New York: Simon & Schuster, 2004, 298.

7. *Inter-Parliamentary Union*. "Equality in Politics: A Survey of Women and Men in Parliaments," 2008, (26) http://www.ipu.org /PDF/publications/equality08-e.pdf.

8. *Amnesty International*. "Russian Federation: Nowhere to turn to: violence against women in the family." Dec. 14, 2005. (1) http://www.amnesty.org/en/library/asset/EUR46/056/2005/en /d61aeef6-d47e-11dd-8743-d305bea2b2c7/eur460562005en.pdf.

9. Obadina, Tunde. "Nigeria's Economy at the Crossroads," *Africa Recovery 13*(1), June 1999, 8. http://www.un.org/ecosocdev/geninfo /afrec/subjindx/subpdfs/131nigr.pdf.

10. *UNICEF*. "The Nigeria Situation." http://www.unicef.org/nigeria /1971_2199.html.

11. Obadina, Tunde. "Nigeria's Economy at the Crossroads," *Africa Recovery 13*(1), June 1999, 8. http://www.un.org/ecosocdev/geninfo /afrec/subjindx/subpdfs/131nigr.pdf.

12. Ibid.

13. Ibid.

14. Ibid.

15. Vera, Dr. Raúl R. "Peru." *Food and Agriculture Organization of the United Nations*. 2006. http://www.fao.org/ag/AGP/AGPC/doc/Coun prof/PDF%20files/Peru_English.pdf.

16. *International Crisis Group (2008)*. "Somalia: To Move Beyond a Failed State." *Africa Report*. (47). http://www.crisisgroup.org/home/index .cfm?id=5836&l=1.

17. *United Nations Population Fund.* "Country Programme Document for Somalia," Executive Board of the United Nations Development Programme and of the United Nations Populations Fund, 2007. Retrieved from http://www.unfpa.org/exbrd/2008/first session/dpfpa_cpd_som_1.pdf.

18. *UNICEF.* "Eastern and Southern Africa – Child Protection Issues." http://www.unicef.org/esaro/5480_child_protection.html.

Chapter 2

1. "Researchers Warn of Impending Disaster from Mass Arsenic Poisoning," *Bulletin of the World Health Organization*, Sept. 2000. http://www.who.int/inf-pr-2000/en/pr2000-55.html.

2. Healy, Ann Marie and Andrew Zolli. "Vision Statement: When Failure Looks Like Success." *Harvard Business Review Magazine.* Apr. 1, 2011.

3. Ibid.

4. "Hillary Rodham Clinton," *New York Times*, Dec. 1, 2011. http://topics.nytimes.com/top/reference/timestopics/people/c/hillary_rodham_clinton/index.html.

5. Eagly, Alice H., and Linda L. Carli. "The Female Leadership Advantage: An Evaluation of the Evidence," *Leadership Quarterly*, 2003, 14, 807–34.

6. *Inter-Parliamentary Union.* "Equality in Politics: A Survey of Women and Men in Parliaments," 2008, (16). http://www.ipu.org/PDF/publications/equality08-e.pdf.

7. Goleman, Daniel. "What Makes a Leader?" *Harvard Business Review,* Nov. 2011, www.hbr.org/2004/01/what-makes-a-leader/ar/pr.

8. *Embassy of the State of Kuwait – Australia and New Zealand.* "The Role of Women in Kuwait." http://www.kuwaitemb-australia.com/women.html.

9. Eltahawy, Mona. "Kuwait rejects political rights for women." *The Guardian.* Nov. 30, 1999. http://www.guardian.co.uk/world/1999/dec/01/1.

10. *Global Security.* "Guatemala Civil War 1960–1996," (3). http://www.globalsecurity.org/military/world/war/guatemala.htm.

11. *Lonely Planet.* "History: Guatemala." http://www.lonelyplanet.com /guatemala/history#160740.

12. "Timeline: Guatemala's History of Violence," *PBS Frontline World.* http://www.pbs.org/frontlineworld/stories/guatemala704/history /timeline.html#.

13. *U.S. Department of State: Bureau of East Asian and Pacific Affairs.* "Background Note: Cambodia." Aug. 10, 2011. http://www.state.gov /r/pa/ei/bgn/2732.htm.

14. *Mu Sochua: MP & Human Rights Advocate.* "Bio." http://sochua .wordpress.com/history/biography/.

15. *CIA* Factbook. "Pakistan." https://www.cia.gov/library/publications /the-world-factbook/geos/pk.html.

16. *US Department of State.* "Background Note: Cameroon." Jan. 1, 2012. http://www.state.gov/r/pa/ei/bgn/26431.htm.

17. *International Monetary Fund.* "Cameroon: Poverty Reduction Strategy Paper." IMF Country Report No. 10/257. Aug 2010. (14–15, 41) http://www.imf.org/external/pubs/ft/scr/2010/cr10257.pdf.

18. Hamano, Aya. "GDP for American Samoa, the Commonwealth of the Northern Mariana Islands, Guam, and the U.S. Virgin Islands." *US Department of Commerce: Bureau of Economic Analysis.* Sept. 2011. (42). http://www.bea.gov/scb/pdf/2011/2009%20September /0911_territories.pdf.

19. *World Health Organization.* "WHO Multi-country Study on Women's Health and Domestic Violence against Women: Samoa." 2005. http://www.who.int/gender/violence/who_multicountry _study/fact_sheets/Samoa2.pdf.

20. *Millennium Development Goals Indicators.* "Seats held by women in national parliament, percentage." Aug. 29, 2011. http://mdgs.un.org /unsd/mdg/SeriesDetail.aspx?srid=557&crid=882.

Chapter 3

1. "Betty Williams—Nobel Lecture." http://www.nobelprize.org /nobel_prizes/peace/laureates/1976/williams-lecture.html.

2. Ibid.

3. Aarvik, Egil. "Award Ceremony Speech," *Nobel Prize,* Dec. 10, 1977. http://www.nobelprize.org/nobel_prizes/peace/laureates /1976/press.html#.

4. Finch, Cristina. "No Woman, No Peace,"*Amnesty International,* Dec. 19, 2011. http://blog.amnestyusa.org/women/no-woman-no -peace/

5. Nye, Joseph S. "When women lead the world," *Al Jazeera,* Feb. 17, 2012. http://www.aljazeera.com/indepth/opinion/2012/02/2012210 75020654159.html?utm_content=automateplus&utm_campaign =Trial6&utm_source=SocialFlow&utm_term=tweets&utm_me dium=MasterAccount.

6. Fisher, Helen. The First Sex: The Natural Talents of Women and How They Are Changing the World, New York: Random House, 1999.

7. Goleman, Daniel. "What Makes a Leader?" *Harvard Business Review,* Nov. 2011. www.hbr.org/2004/01/what-makes-a-leader/ar/pr.

8. Eagly, Alice H., Mary C. Johannesen-Schmidt, and Marloes L. van Engen. "Transformational, Transactional, and Laissez-Faire Leadership Styles: A Meta-Analysis Comparing Women and Men," *Psychological Bulletin 129*(4), 2003, 569–91.

9. Burke, Sarah and Karen M. Collins. "Gender Differences in Leadership Styles and Management Skills," *Women In Management Review, 16*(5), pp. 244–257, 2001 Rosener, J. B. "Ways Women Lead," *Harvard Business Review, 68*(6), 119–125, 1990 Fine, Marlene G. "Women, Collaboration, and Social Change: An Ethics Based Model of Leadership," in *Women and Leadership: Visions and Diverse Voices,* ed. Jean Lau Chin, Betrice Lott, Joy K. Rice, and Janis Sanchez-Hucles, 177–91. Boston: Blackwell, 2008.

10. Summers, Chris. "Lives lost to the Troubles."*BBC News.* Jan. 28, 2009. http://news.bbc.co.uk/2/hi/7853266.stm.

11. Kershner, Isabel. "Elusive Line Defines Lives in Israel and the West Bank." *The New York Times.* Sept. 6, 2011. http://www.ny times.com/2011/09/07/world/middleeast/07borders.html?pagewan ted=all.

12. *The Sixth African Development Forum.* "Achieving gender equality and women's empowerment in Africa Progress Report." Nov.

19–21, 2008. (23). http://www.uneca.org/adfvi/documents/ADFVI _Progress_Report_ENG.pdf.

13. "Women: A Work Never Done," *The Economist Online*, Mar. 8, 2011. http://www.economist.com/blogs/dailychart/2011/03/women.

14. *The Sixth African Development Forum*. "Achieving gender equality and women's empowerment in Africa Progress Report." Nov. 19–21, 2008. (22). http://www.uneca.org/adfvi/documents/ADFVI _Progress_Report_ENG.pdf.

15. Coleman, Isobel. "The Better Half." *Foreign Affairs*. Jan/Feb 2010. http://www.foreignaffairs.com/articles/65728/isobel-coleman/the -better-half?page=show.

16. *Health Poverty Action*. "Success Stories: Using Radio to improve health education." http://www.healthpovertyaction.org/where-we -work/africa/rwanda/radio/.

Chapter 4

1. Gbowee, Leymah. "Nobel Lecture," *Nobel Prize*, Dec. 10, 2011. http: //www.nobelprize.org/nobel_prizes/peace/laureates/2011/gbowee -lecture_en.html.

2. Sirleaf, Ellen Johnson. "Nobel Lecture," *Nobel Prize*, Dec. 10, 2011. http://www.nobelprize.org/nobel_prizes/peace/laureates/2011/john son_sirleaf-lecture_en.html.

3. *U.S. Department of State, Bureau of African Affairs*. "Background Note: Liberia," Nov. 22, 2011. http://www.state.gov/r/pa/ei/bgn /6618.htm.

4. Karman, Tawakkol. "Nobel Lecture," *Nobel Prize*, Dec. 10, 2011. http://www.nobelprize.org/nobel_prizes/peace/laureates/2011/kar man-lecture_en.html.

5. Maxfield, Sylvia, Mary Shapiro, Vipin Gupta, and Susan Hass. "Gender and Risk: Women, Risk Taking and Risk Aversion," *Gender in Management: An International Journal 25*(7), 2010, 586–604.

6. *U.S. Department of State, Bureau of Western Hemisphere Affairs*. "Background Note: Argentina," Mar. 12, 2012. http://www .state.gov/r/pa/ei/bgn/26516.htm.

7. *BBC News*. "Argentine Mothers Mark 30 Years." Apr. 30, 2007. http: //news.bbc.co.uk/2/hi/americas/6608871.stm.

8. Boustany, Nora. "As Ukraine Watched the Party Line, She Took the Truth into Her Hands," *Washington Post*, Apr. 29, 2005. http://www.washingtonpost.com/wp-dyn/content/article/2005/04/28/AR2005042801696.html.

9. Ibid.

10. *National Democratic Institute.* "Campaign Schools Prepare Egyptian Women to Run for Office." Sept. 29, 2011. http://www.ndi.org/campaign-schools-Egypt.

11. Ryan, Michelle K., and S. Alexander Haslam. "The Glass Cliff: Evidence That Women Are Over-Represented in Precarious Leadership Positions," *British Journal of Management*, 16, 81–90, 2005.

12. Mather, Mara, Nicole R. Lighthall, Lin Nga, and Marissa A. Gorlick. "Sex Differences in How Stress Affects Brain Activity During Face Viewing," *Neuroreport 21*(14), 2010, 933–37. Accessed Aug. 15, 2011, doi:10.1097/WNR.0b013e32833ddd92.

13. Hossain, Dr. Naomi, and Dr. Celestine Nyamu Musembi. "Corruption, Accountability and Gender: Understanding the Connections." United Nations Development Fund for Women. 2010.

14. *Centers for Disease Control and Prevention.* (Footnote.) "Understanding Intimate Partner Violence," 2012. http://www.cdc.gov/ViolencePrevention/pdf/IPV_Factsheet-a.pdf.

15. *U.S. Department of State, Bureau of Western Hemisphere Affairs.* "Background Note: Argentina," Mar. 12, 2012. http://www.state.gov/r/pa/ei/bgn/26516.htm.

16. Anderson, Lisa. "TRUSTLAW POLL – Afghanistan Is Most Dangerous Country for Women." *TrustLaw Women*, Jun. 15, 2011. http://www.trust.org/trustlaw/news/trustlaw-poll-afghanistan-is-most-dangerous-country-for-women.

17. *International Rescue Committee.* "Measuring Mortality in the Democratic Republic of Congo." http://www.rescue.org/sites/default/files/resource-file/IRC_DRCMortalityFacts.pdf.

18. "DR Congo Mass Rape Verdicts Send Strong Signal to Perpetrators—UN envoy," UN News Centre, Feb. 21, 2011, http://www.un.org/apps/news/story.asp?NewsID=37580&Cr=sexual.

Chapter 5

1. Fisher, Helen E. "The Natural Leadership Talents of Women." In *Enlightened Power: How Women Are Transforming the Practice of Leadership*, edited by Linda Coughlin, Ellen Wingard, and Keith Hollihan, 133–40. San Francisco: Jossey-Bass, 2005.

2. *USAID: Swaziland*. "HIV/AIDS Health Profile," Oct. 2010. http://www.usaid.gov/our_work/global_health/aids/Countries/africa/swaziland_profile.pdf.

3. *USAID: Swaziland*. "HIV/AIDS Health Profile," Oct. 2010. http://www.usaid.gov/our_work/global_health/aids/Countries/africa/swaziland_profile.pdf.

4. Burt, Ronald S. "The Network Structure of Social Capital." *Research in Organizational Behavior*. Volume 22, *(345–423)* 2000. http://jaylee.business.ku.edu/MGMT%20916/PDF/The%20Network%20Structure%20of%20Social%20Capital.pdf.

5. Carter, Nancy M., Herminia Ibarra, and Christine Silva. "Why Men Still Get More Promotions than Women: Your High-Potential Females Need More than Just Well-Meaning Mentors," *Harvard Business Review*, Sept. 2010, http://static.ow.ly/docs/HBR Why Men Still Get More Promotions Than Women_6s5.pdf.

6. Ragins, Belle Rose, and Terri A. Scandura. "Burden or Blessing? Expected Costs and Benefits of Being a Mentor," *Journal of Organizational Behavior* 20(4), July 1999, 493–509.

7. FED became a model for women around the world and particularly in the region, where ten local Vital Voices chapters throughout the Americas have enabled the women we have served to reach thousands more women and develop leaders locally. From 2000 to 2006, Vital Voices trained and supported 2,700 women globally. Working in collaboration with our chapters, in 2010 alone we were able to train and support that same number, just in Latin America.

8. *CIA World Factbook*. "Background Note: Haiti." Feb. 21, 2012. https://www.cia.gov/library/publications/the-world-factbook/geos/ha.html.

9. Ibid.

10. Nandal, Santosh. "Extent and Causes of Gender and Poverty in India: A Case Study of Rural Hayana," *Journal of International Women's Studies* 7(2), Nov. 2005.

11. *UN News Centre*. "Tens of millions to benefit from India's Right to Education Act—UN agencies." Apr. 3, 2010. http://www.un .org/apps/news/story.asp?Cr=education&Cr1=&NewsID=34273.

12. *The World Bank*. "2012 World Development Report: Gender Equality and Development." 2012 (152). http://siteresources .worldbank.org/INTWDR2012/Resources/7778105-1299699968583 /7786210-1315936222006/Complete-Report.pdf.

Conclusion

1. Yi, Matthew. "Young Berkeley Journalists Broke Landlord Story Early." *SFGate*. Jan. 21, 2000. http://www.sfgate.com/cgi-bin/article .cgi?f=/e/a/2000/01/21/NEWS13537.dtl.

2. *Girls Not Brides*. "Key Facts," 2002. http://girlsnotbrides.org/child -marriage/.

3. *The Elders*. "Girls Not Brides—A New Global Partnership to End Child Marriage." Sept. 20, 2011. http://theelders.org/he/article/girls -not-brides-new-global-partnership-end-child-marriage.

ACKNOWLEDGMENTS

This book and these lessons in leadership were inspired by a seventeen-year journey around the world and by the women we've worked with along the way who have touched our lives and shaped the work of Vital Voices. What we learned from them made Vital Voices a better organization; better able to support and stand behind other women around the world. Our goal with this book is to share those lessons as widely as we can, in the hopes that others who aspire to make a difference will draw inspiration, guidance, and determination from the voices, stories, and achievements of the women we have known. At the beginning of this process, many people told me it would be next to impossible to write a book while running a fast-growing organization. In truth, I found the process of recounting the stories of these remarkable leaders deeply energizing. It reaffirmed the power of this new model of leadership. Writing down these stories as I continued to travel the globe to work with the Vital Voices women leaders pushed me further, instilling each chapter with new inspiration. First and foremost, I must thank the remarkable leaders who agreed to let me share their stories through the pages of this book. It is an honor for us to stand behind them.

A heartfelt thank-you to our founder Hillary Rodham Clinton for her vision and leadership. I admire her most for what she taught me in Beijing: true leaders seek voice and power to empower others. And to former Secretary of State Madeleine Albright. These two women never hesitate to speak for those who have no voice. They have been using their platforms to advance the role of women in our world long before it was fashionable, mainstream, or even acceptable to do so. For that, we are enormously grateful.

One of the greatest lessons I have learned from my work with Vital Voices is that the best results come from collaboration. This book is no exception. A huge thank-you must go to my chief collaborators: Aaron Kisner, Alyson Wise, and Lauren Wollack. Their editing, brainstorming, and constant encouragement and support throughout the process was invaluable. Aaron, Vital Voices' creative director and one of the most brilliant storytellers I know, helped channel the Vital Voices women leaders. Alyson and Lauren, who have both worked with Vital Voices for many years, helped bring our leadership model to life.

I thank my partners Susan Davis, our board chair, and Bobbie Greene McCarthy, our vice chair, for their generosity, extraordinary commitment to Vital Voices, and deep devotion to the women we serve. I have learned so much working alongside these two smart and wonderfully talented women. Their support of me, and this project from its inception, provided tremendous encouragement.

Thank you to Karen Murphy, my editor and her team at Jossey-Bass/Wiley. Karen believed in this project from day one. I so appreciate her advice and editing, every step of the way. Without her gentle—and when needed, not so gentle—prodding and cheering, I may have never crossed the finish line.

Many thanks must also go to Vinca LaFleur, Sarada Peri, and Julia Lam who carefully read and edited drafts and pushed me to dig deeper.

I am a product of Vital Voices. I will never be able to pay back Melanne Verveer and Mary Delay Yerrick for their years of investing in me. The only thing I can do is promise to "pay forward" the multitude of hours they spent mentoring, preparing, and believing in me. As our chair and vice chair emeritus and former co-CEOs, they built Vital Voices from the ground up. Their tireless efforts and selfless commitment to the women we serve charted a course for me to follow.

Thank you to Vital Voices honorary cochairs Senator Kay Bailey Hutchison and former Senator Nancy Kassebaum Baker for their leadership and support of Vital Voices over the years. And many thanks to our co-founder former Secretary of State Madeleine Albright for consistently speaking truth to power and advancing the agenda for women around the globe. And to former First Lady Laura Bush, a staunch advocate for women in some of the darkest corners of the world, for her leadership and friendship.

To the leaders who inspired each chapter of this book with their words of wisdom: they each infuse everything they do with passion and a commitment to women's progress. I must thank Vital Voices board member, businesswoman, and designer Diane von Furstenberg for her bold vision and constant generosity; board member emeritus and Nigeria's minister of finance Ngozi Okonjo-Iweala for her courageous example; Vital Voices board member and actress Sally Field for her unwavering support from our earliest days; and former president of Chile and executive director of UN Women Michelle Bachelet for her exemplary leadership.

To the founding mothers and first board members of Vital Voices—tried-and-true supporters of the organization and treasured mentors—Judith McHale, Donna Cochran McLarty, and Marylouise Oates. The entire Vital Voices board of directors deserves special recognition for their profound dedication to our work and generously giving their time, expertise, and resources: Jaspal Bindra, Beth Brooke, Paul Charron, Tia Cudahy, Debbie Dingell, Ambassador Paula J. Dobriansky, Sonnie Dockser, Samia Farouki, Mary C. Foerster, Nancy Folger, Baroness Mary Goudie, Kate James, Ambassador Craig Johnstone, Dr. Alice Kandell, Dr. Carol Lancaster, Marlene Malek, Suzanne McCarron, V. Sue Molina, Susan Ness, Dr. Karen Otazo Hofmeister, Dina Habib Powell, Nancy Prager-Kamel, Victoria Sant, Roselyne Swig, and Kathleen Vaughan. I also want to pay tribute to Vital Voices board members emeritus who remain involved and extremely supportive of our work: Ambassador Elizabeth Frawley Bagley, Betty Bumpers, Dr. Jill Iscol, and Jan Piercy. Thank you to Theresa Loar, Vital Voices founding president, for her dedication and leadership of Vital Voices in our formative years. I also want to thank her personally for taking a chance on me back in 1996. And to the remarkable Ambassador Swanee Hunt, who developed the Vital Voices concept, came up with the name, and hosted the first conference in 1997, which ignited a movement. My gratitude for all she has done to push forward the rights and opportunities of women around the world.

At Vital Voices I am blessed to work alongside an extraordinary team of smart, passionate, and wonderful women and men. Thanks to the entire team at Vital Voices for all the work they do each day with energy, grace, and humility. To Kathy Hendrix for remaining such a valuable partner and true friend over the course of this journey. Her imprint has touched so many aspects of the organization, including this book, and her wit and wisdom have made every endeavor more interesting. Thanks to Vital Voices' brilliant strategic communications team, led by Vice President Margaux Bergen and including Ann Hoffman, Vikki Loles, and Katie Stanton, and to our director of strategic partnerships Jenny Morris, for their support throughout this entire process. I particularly want to thank Vikki for her commitment to this book—reading, editing, and providing thoughtful feedback every step of the way. Thanks too to Annie Hurwitz, a master sleuth who tracked down information and photos, scheduled interviews, and generally kept me on deadline with all the final details. Thanks also to those who conducted research for the book: Carey Hogg and Emily Edgecombe. To the insightful Mayra Buvinic, who we are honored to call a Vital Voices senior fellow, for her wisdom and advice. A heartfelt thank-you to all the Vital Voices staff who provided feedback and assistance in many different ways: Sophia Aziz, Maya Babla, Dereje Belay, Julia Billings, Chris Carr, Bernadette Castillo, Vicki Cate, Ashley Chandler, Liam Dall, Cindy Dyer, Christie Edwards, Sarah Ewing, Rebecca Ganster, Christine German, Celena Green, Yaba Haffar, Nicole Hauspurg, Emma Hersh, Dinah Jean, Daphna Kapnik, Mary

MacPherson, Eniola Mafe, Shelby Merkel, Melissa Morales, Jennifer Morris, Kathrine Nasteva, Malini Patel, Maria Peña, Eugenia Podesta, Gillian Robinson, Helah Robinson, Melysa Sperber, Kianoosh Tahbaz-Salehi, Sandra Taylor, Sara Vandepeute, and Mekdes Woldemariam.

Partnership is part of our DNA at Vital Voices. Many thanks to our most valued partners, including the magnificent Tina Brown for using her power and platform to shine a spotlight on women's issues around the world, and to her dynamic team at Women in the World, particularly Kim Azzerelli and Kyle Gibson. To Suzanne McCarron and her team at ExxonMobil, particularly Beth Snyder and Lorie Jackson whose strategic advice and leadership helped us build a best-in-class Global Businesswomen's Network to support women entrepreneurs around the world. I must thank Pattie Sellers and her team at *Fortune* and Chris Miner and the U.S. State Department for our collaboration in developing the Fortune / State Department Global Mentoring Partnership. Many thanks to Anne Finucane for her visionary leadership and to our other partners at Bank of America, particularly Rena Desisto, Pam Seagle, and Kathleen Brady, in developing our Global Ambassadors Program to close the leadership gap for women around the world. To the dynamic Kay Krill and our partners at Ann Inc., particularly Catherine Fischer, for our innovative partnership around ANNpower, a program to empower young women as leaders with a global vision. And to Dina Powell and Noa Meyer, our partners at Goldman Sachs's 10,000 Women for leading the way and being such loyal partners and friends for so many years. To Carol Kurzig and her team at the Avon Foundation, who have been instrumental in forging the Global Partnership to End Violence Against Women with us. To our partners at Walmart, particularly Susan Chambers, Sylvia Mathews Burwell, Leslie Dach, and Sarah Thorn. To the Dutch Ministry for Foreign Affairs, the World Bank, Australian AID, and New Zealand Aid, most especially Amanda Ellis for her leadership and extraordinary commitment. I am grateful to the Clinton Global Initiative and its founder and moving force President Bill Clinton for using his unique position and global spotlight to illuminate the plight of too many of the world's women.

A huge thank-you to those who have invested their time and generous resources in our work, particularly Paul E. Singer and Annie Dickerson of the Paul Singer Foundation and Omidyar. Many thanks to our friends and partners at New York University: Bob Shrum, Rogan Kersh, and Ellyn Toscano. And special thanks to Luisella Meloni and the team at Diane von Furstenberg; we treasure this invaluable partnership. I also want to acknowledge Cindi Leive, Susan Goodall, and our partners at *Glamour Magazine* for bringing global women's issues into the mainstream.

A special thank you to Philippe Reines for his continued support of this project. And to Marlin Dohlman and Whitney Allgood for expert advice. I also want to thank Andrew Zolli, Leetha Filderman, and their team at PopTech for their inspiration and making it possible for Karen Murphy and me to meet and conceive of this project.

A special shout out to the magnificent men who have believed in Vital Voices and supported our work in big and small ways behind the scenes since our founding days:

John Yerrick, Phil Verveer, Thomas "Mack" McLarty, and Patrick McCarthy.

I am grateful to the dedicated members of the Vital Voices Global Advisory Council members, many of whom are featured in this book for their partnerships and commitment over the years.

To our Vital Voices Connecticut Council, led by Roberta Cooper, for their devotion to the women in the Vital Voices Network. To Carol Mack and each of the playwrights Paula Cizmar, Catherine Filloux, Gail Kriegel, Ruth Margraff, Anna Deavere Smith, and Susan Yankowitz, who brought the stories of several Vital Voices women leaders to life on the stage in the much admired, globe-trotting play *Seven*.

A huge thank-you to the Vital Voices chapter and affiliate leaders and those who lead Vital Voices businesswomen's networks around the world: Sheila Amdany, board member, Kenya Association of Women Business Owners (KAWBO); Juliet Asante, president, Eagle Women's Empowerment Club (EWEC); Adeola Azeez, chairperson, Women in Management and Business of Nigeria (WIMBIZ); Mabel Kiggundu, board member, Uganda Women Entrepreneurs Association Limited (UWEAL); Kunyalala Maphisa, president, Business Women's Association of South Africa (BWASA); Eva Muraya, president, KAWBO; Jennifer Mwijukye, president, UWEAL; Pauline Ofong, board member, UWEAL; and Funmi Roberts, board member, WIMBIZ; Amal Al Masri, board member, Palestinian Businesswomen Forum; Faiza Al Sayed, vice president, Dubai Business Women Council; Afnan Al Zayani, board member, Bahrain Businesswomen Society; Aisha Al Fardan, vice chairwoman,

Qatari Businesswomen Association; Shereen Allam, president, Association for Women's Total Advancement and Development (Egypt); Khalida Azbane, vice president and executive board member, Association des Femmes Chefs D'Enterprise du Maroc (Morocco); Khedidja Belhadi, president, Algériennes Managers et Entrepreneurs; Amel Bouchamaoui, first vice president, Chambre Nationale des Femmes Chefs d'Entreprises (Tunisia); Lana Dajani, member, Business and Professional Women's Association (Jordan); and Hanan Saab, president, Lebanese League for Women in Business; Carmen Irene Alas, co-founder and president, Voces Vitales El Salvador; Nadege Beauvil, president, Femmes en Démocratie; Maria Eugenia Brizuela, co-founder and vice president, Voces Vitales El Salvador; Laura Busnelli, co-founder and treasurer, Voces Vitales Argentina; Cristiana Chamorro, co-founder, Voces Vitales Nicaragua; Mercedes Deshon, co-founder, Voces Vitales Nicaragua; Clarisa Eseiza, co-founder, Voces Vitales Argentina; Sylvia Gereda, co-founder and president of the board, Voces Vitales Guatemala; Ana Goldman, executive director, Voces Vitales Argentina; Johanna Hill, copresident, Voces Vitales El Salvador; Maria Gabriela Hoch, co-founder and president, Voces Vitales Argentina; Candice Lloyd, co-founder, Voces Vitales Honduras; Claudia Patricia Luna, president, Elas por Elas: Vozes e Ações das Mulheres; Daniela Martin, board member, Voces Vitales Argentina; Cecilia Martinez, executive director, Voces Vitales Honduras; Marie Carmel Michaud, executive director, Femmes en Démocratie; Reyna McPeck, founder, Voces Vitales Venezuela; Ana Maria Osorio, executive director, Voces

Vitales El Salvador; Maria Pacheco, co-founder, Voces Vitales Guatemala; Lorena Piazze, co-founder, Voces Vitales Argentina; Gisela Porras, president, Voces Vitales Panamá; Maria Nelly Rivas, co-founder, Voces Vitales Nicaragua; Maria Liliana Ruiz, executive director, Voces Vitales Guatemala; Danielle Saint-Lot, co-founder, Femmes en Démocratie; Anne-Valerie Timothee Milfort, co-founder, Femmes en Démocratie; Mabel Velasquez, co-founder, Voces Vitales Honduras; Egda Velez, co-founder, Voces Vitales Nicaragua; Annie Vial, executive director, Voces Vitales Panamá; Isis Vivas, executive director, Voces Vitales Venezuela; Regina Wong, co-founder, Voces Vitales Honduras; Gladys Zarak, founder and president, Voces Vitales Perú; and Ana Zavala Hanon, executive director, Voces Vitales Nicaragua.

Many thanks to the deeply valued former Vital Voices staff and advisors who helped to shape the organization: Anita Botti, Steve Warnath, Wenchi Yu, Laura Ardito, Alvin Allgood, Zoe Dean Smith, and former president Sandra Willett Jackson. And to early Vital Voices trainers and mentors Stephenie Foster, Karin Shipman, Jill Schuker, and Mary Davis Holt. And to those who have dedicated their lives to this cause, pushing the debate forward through their writing and their work: Isobel Coleman and Gayle Tzemach Lemmon at the Council on Foreign Relations, and Pulitzer Prize-winning authors Nick Kristof and Sheryl WuDunn. Special thanks to the leaders we admire so much working to advance the cause of women: Zainab Salbi, founder of Women for Women, for her leadership; Pat Michell, CEO of the Paley Center for Media; Elizabeth Vazquez, president,

CEO, and co-founder, WEConnect International; and Ritu Sharma, president and co-founder, Women Thrive Worldwide. And to all the great advocates for leaders who have given their lives to this important work.

I so appreciate those who lent their artistic talents to this book by photographing the women leaders profiled throughout these pages: Aaron Kisner, Kate Cummings, Micky Wiswedel, Maria Soshenko, Sharon Farmer, the Ministry of Women Affairs of Peru, Josh Cogan, Amy Drucker, PressEye Photography Northern Ireland, Clinton Global Initiative, Alexander Ivshin, Peace Boat, Liu Yulin, Chris Wright, Kolkata Sanved Archive, P. Rajeswari, Shiza Shahid, and Lisa Nipp.

And to the extraordinary Michele Bohana for helping us to complete this powerful journey.

On a personal note, I have to thank my amazing family, John and Mary, my parents, and Jay, Heather, Rachel, David, and Nala, for instilling in me an insatiable curiosity and a passion to change the world; the courage and entrepreneurial spirit to make my own path; and the comfort of always knowing that someone believes in the beauty of my dreams. And to Hardin Lang for his patience and support always.

ALYSE NELSON is president and chief executive officer of Vital Voices Global Partnership. A co-founder of Vital Voices, Alyse has worked for the organization for fifteen years, serving as vice president and senior director of programs before assuming her current role in 2009. Alyse has worked with women leaders to develop training programs and international forums in over 140 countries and has interviewed more than 200 international leaders, including Liberian president Ellen Johnson Sirleaf and former presidents Mary Robinson and Bill Clinton, as well as Nobel Peace Prize laureates Aung San Suu Kyi, Wangari Maathai, and Muhammad Yunus. Under her leadership, Vital Voices has tripled in size and expanded its global reach to serve a network of over twelve thousand women leaders in 144 countries.

Previously, Alyse served as deputy director of the Vital Voices Global Democracy Initiative at the U.S. Department of State. Her position aided former First Lady Hillary Clinton and Secretary of State Madeleine Albright's commitment to promote the advancement of women as a U.S. foreign policy objective. Alyse helped design and implement Vital Voices initiatives throughout the world. From July 1996 to July 2000, Alyse worked with the President's Interagency Council on Women at the White House and U.S. Department of State. She attended the UN Fourth World Conference on Women in Beijing, China, in 1995. She serves on Secretary Clinton's Advisory Committee on Strategic Dialogue with Civil Society and is a board member of Running Start.

Alyse has been featured in international and national media, including the *Washington Post*, *Financial Times*, the *Miami Herald*, the *Wall Street Journal*, *USA Today*, and Reuters, and has appeared on BBC, PBS, CNN, NPR, Fox News, and CNBC. She completed her graduate degree work at the Fletcher School of Law and Diplomacy at Tufts University. In 2006 Alyse was named one of "Ten Women to Watch" by *Washingtonian Magazine*, was honored by her alma mater, Emerson College, with the Distinguished Speaker award, and in 2011 she was featured in *Newsweek* as one of "150 Women Shaking the World."

• • •

VITAL VOICES GLOBAL PARTNERSHIP is an international nongovernmental organization that identifies, trains, mentors, and provides visibility to innovative women leaders who advance development in ways that benefit society as a whole. Founded by U.S. Secretary of State Hillary Clinton in 1997, Vital Voices invests in women's leadership as a vehicle for transformative change in economic development and entrepreneurship, human rights, and political and public leadership.

For more information, please visit www.vitalvoices.org.